THE WOMAN'S PUBLIC SPEAKING HANDBOOK

Elizabeth J. Natalle
The University of North Carolina at Greensboro

Fritzi R. Bodenheimer
Montgomery College

Australia • Canada • Mexico • Singapore • Spain • United Kingdom • United States

COPYRIGHT © 2004 Wadsworth, a division of Thomson Learning, Inc. Thomson Learning™ is a trademark used herein under license.

ALL RIGHTS RESERVED. No part of this work covered by the copyright hereon may be reproduced or used in any form or by any means—graphic, electronic, or mechanical, including but not limited to photocopying, recording, taping, Web distribution, information networks, or information storage and retrieval systems—without the written permission of the publisher.

Printed in Canada
1 2 3 4 5 6 7 07 06 05 04 03

Printer: Webcom Limited

ISBN: 0-534-59886-2

For more information about our products, contact us at:
Thomson Learning
Academic Resource Center
1-800-423-0563

For permission to use material from this text, contact us by:
Phone: 1-800-730-2214
Fax: 1-800-731-2215
Web: http://www.thomsonrights.com

Wadsworth/Thomson Learning
10 Davis Drive
Belmont, CA 94002-3098
USA

Asia
Thomson Learning
5 Shenton Way #01-01
UIC Building
Singapore 068808

Australia/New Zealand
Thomson Learning
102 Dodds Street
Southbank, Victoria 3006
Australia

Canada
Nelson
1120 Birchmount Road
Toronto, Ontario M1K 5G4
Canada

Europe/Middle East/South Africa
Thomson Learning
High Holborn House
50/51 Bedford Row
London WC1R 4LR
United Kingdom

Latin America
Thomson Learning
Seneca, 53
Colonia Polanco
11560 Mexico D.F.
Mexico

Spain/Portugal
Paraninfo
Calle/Magallanes, 25
28015 Madrid, Spain

TABLE OF CONTENTS

Acknowledgments	vi
Introduction	1
Purposes of the Handbook	2
Intended Readers	7
Preview of the Chapters	7
Special Features	8
Meet the Authors	9
Chapter One	
Preparing the Message	**13**
Getting Organized	13
What Does Gender Have to Do With It?	14
Chapter Two	
Relating to the Audience	**23**
Researching an Audience	23
Traditional Audience Analysis	25
Nontraditional Audience Analysis	28
Occasion and Audience Mind-Set	31
Preparing for a Hostile Audience	32
Meeting the Hostile Audience	36
Working an Audience	38
Working With an Audience Over Time	46
Chapter Three	
Delivering the Message	**49**
Gender and Credibility	50
Before the Speech	52
Conquering Stage Fright	53

Take a Deep Breath	58
I Haven't Got a Thing to Wear	59
During the Speech	63
Stand Up Straight	63
Speak Up	65
Create Connection	67
The Podium as a Gender Problem	68
After the Speech	70

Chapter Four
Tools of the Trade: Delivery Resources   73

The World of Gendered Technology	74
Getting Equipped	79
Traditional or High Tech?	79
Traditional Tools	80
Technological Tools	81
Microphones	83
The Tools of Mass Media	85
Language	88
The Gender-Linked Language Effect	89
Gendered Humor	90
Qualifiers and Tag Questions	91
Neutral Language	92

Chapter Five
Public Speaking Situations   95

Special Occasions	96
Making an Introduction	96
Giving or Receiving an Award	99
Giving a Toast	101
Sharing Expertise on Panels	102
Public Speaking in the Workplace	105
Giving a Report	106
Meeting Mania	107
Training	108

Chapter Six
Woman as Public Persona — 113

    Obliteration and Objectification — 114
    Feminine Style on the Campaign Trail — 117
    First Ladies — 119
    Queens and Prime Ministers — 122
    Women of Color — 124
    Negotiating Persona With Your Public — 127
    The Media Factor — 129
    Prepare a Media Kit — 132
    Gender Identity Politics — 133

Epilogue — 137

    Self-Diagnosis and Action Plan — 137
    The Woman Speaker's Ten Rules for Success—Two Versions — 140
        Jody's Rules — 140
        Fritzi's Rules — 141

Bibliography — 143

Pullout Tools — 155

    Presentation Checklist — 155
    Speech Outline Template — 157
    Audience Analysis Checklist — 160
    Sources for Further Study — 161

Journal Notes — 163

Index — 165

Acknowledgments

We wish to thank the people who kindly and expertly helped this project from start to finish. First, thanks to our students and the many organizations that have given us a forum to teach and practice public speaking. To Tracy Landrum, thank you for passing our manuscript on to Wadsworth for consideration. We also thank Executive Editor Deirdre Anderson, Editorial Assistant Amber Fawson, and Copyeditor Kate Dragolovich for their hard work in getting the manuscript to press. Our gratitude goes to Jeanne Goldberg, R. Scott Hengen and Tim Barkley for their special contributions. We appreciate all that has been done to make *The Woman's Public Speaking Handbook* a book we are proud to offer.

Introduction

Public speaking is an integral part of most people's lives. Whether you serve as the president of a student council or as a member of the local school board, speaking in public to diverse audiences is the way you build community and make decisions. As professionals in the field of communication, the authors of this handbook train people to speak, and we, ourselves, engage in public speaking. Our experience tells us that speaking on the public platform is often a different experience for women than it is for men, yet the concept of a gendered public speaker is missing from most modern public speaking training. In reality, an audience notices the gender of a speaker and uses that information as part of a response to the speaker. It is imperative to attend to this fact in public speaking training.

We are not the first authors to come up with the idea of a public speaking handbook for women. Training women to speak publicly has historical precedence. Handbooks from the 1930s include Eudora Ramsay Richardson's *The Woman Speaker* (1936) and J. V. Garland's *Public Speaking for Women* (1938). The authors of these handbooks were aware of the role women could and did play in the formation of public life. Almost seventy years later, we offer a handbook designed to meet the needs of women who still lack the skills and experience that make an effective speaker. Times have certainly changed. For example, the advent of high technology calls for new approaches to the teaching and practice of public speaking. But times also remain the same, as evidenced by Ms. Richardson's quote in the accompanying box. Therefore, we take the opportunity throughout this book to remind you about the history of women on the public platform. We firmly believe that knowing one's history provides a context for making good choices in the present.

> *The woman who would speak acceptably need have only two essentials: something worth saying and an easy manner of saying that something. The one we frequently possess; the other we may certainly acquire.*
>
> Eudora Ramsay Richardson
> Author of *The Woman Speaker*, 1936

Purposes of the Handbook

We live in an interesting historical time with regard to women in public life and the impact of public speaking on national issues. When the 108th United States Congress convened in January 2003, a record fourteen women were sworn in as senators, and fifty-nine women took the oath of office in the House of Representatives ("House Welcomes," 2003; CAWP, 2003). These numbers indicate that women's participation in public life is on the rise. However, women's voices still aren't heard as political leaders, according to The White House Project, a program operated by the nonprofit Women's Leadership Fund. Their study entitled "Who's Talking?" (2001) reports that only 10 percent of the national experts on Sunday political talk shows are women, and that women only account for 6 to 7 percent of repeat guests. The study concludes that such underrepresentation leads to the public perception that women have less knowledge or ability to address political topics than men. This is a real dilemma and reason enough to consider developing your own public speaking skills. It is a matter we took into consideration when thinking about undertaking this book project. In fact, we wrote this handbook for three reasons.

First, we wish to share prescriptions for helping women become effective public speakers. The tradition of public speaking in the United States has largely been a male enterprise. Early training at the nation's first university, Harvard, was designed to give future lawyers, politicians, and ministers the necessary skills to persuade.

Our society's heavy reliance on an Aristotelian, agonistic style of communicating on the public platform has benefited many male speakers. Women, however, have generally experienced difficulty in accommodating to this argumentative, or adversarial, style of speaking. As a result, many women do not participate in debate or public speaking classes and graduate from high school or college without the skills necessary for participation in community life. Catherine Helen Palczewski (1996), a professor of communication, reports that recent research in the field of argumentation indicates that there is a second type of argument—a nonadversarial, or consensual, style—and that this style is often preferred by women. Both the adversarial and nonadversarial styles of public speaking have merit and will be discussed throughout the handbook. We believe that even the most apprehensive speaker should find our discussion useful in regard to making appropriate choices about personal style.

Speaking of apprehension, the second reason for writing this handbook was to help women overcome the fear of public speaking. We believe that there is a tradition of socializing women into believing that they cannot and should not take risks on the public platform. In 1973, early in her career as a spokesperson for the American women's movement, Gloria Steinem gave a speech that contained the following remarks:

> One initial problem for me was learning to speak in public. That's a great problem, I think, for women in general. I notice that in classrooms the pattern still prevails of women who do very well on examinations and don't speak up in class. So, one of the things I'd like to say is that if I can do it, you can do it. If I can do it, anybody can. I never stood up in public in my life until three years ago. I've never gotten accustomed to it. I still get terribly nervous, but you do learn that you don't die. (Laughter) So I hope that more and more women will be standing up and speaking out. (Steinem, 1984)

Although Gloria Steinem (1998) now appears much more comfortable with her public speaking skills (she is, in fact, an excellent speaker who employs humor, good pacing, and appropriate language choices), we continue to notice both popular and academic references to women's fear of speaking. A *Vogue* magazine article from 1987 entitled "Fear of

Speaking" advised women on the corporate fast track to improve their speaking skills by signing up for coaching or joining Toastmasters International (Nonkin, 1987). A study reported in *Business Week* magazine (Weisul, 2002) claims that anxiety levels differ most for professional people who only have to speak in public on occasion. In this situation, 42 percent of women reported high levels of apprehension compared to 15 percent of men. Communication professor Marjorie Jaasma (1997) documented the apprehension levels of female students in the college classroom. Her research reinforced the notion that the higher levels of fear experienced by women when speaking out, as compared to men, may be linked to lower self-esteem. We want to help women dispel the myth that they are not worthy or capable of speaking in public arenas. Every woman has a voice, and every woman has the right to express herself without fear. This handbook will help you overcome apprehension because we reinforce the idea that public speaking is actually a set of skills that can be built in a systematic way. Using both this supplemental text and the main speaking text it accompanies, you will be set for a foray into the public arena.

We hope that you will have the opportunity to experience, as author Susan Faludi has, what happens when you conquer this fear: "I knew public speaking was important to reform public life—but I hadn't realized the transformative effect it could have on the speaker herself. Women need to be heard not just to change the world, but to change themselves" (1992a, p. 29). Faludi (1992b) has also shared her thoughts on how writing and speaking should work together as forms of personal expression: "Since the book [*Backlash*] came out, I've done a great deal of public speaking, and I think that that has been part of my own personal feminist evolution as well, to be able not only to project my voice on paper, but to stand up at a public forum and speak up. It's an extremely liberating experience for women, who are not taught that it's ladylike to take a stand in public."

The third reason for writing this book was to extend our readers' skills beyond the purely technical aspects of public speaking to develop a public persona. It is not enough to know how to write and deliver a speech. In the fast-paced, competitive world we live in, speakers must be noticed and attended to before any speech will achieve its intended goals; therefore, a speaker must develop a public image, or persona, that will be recognized and accepted by a constituency. For example, public figures such as Faye Wattleton, Carol Moseley-Braun, Patricia Schroeder, Maxine Waters, Barbara Mikulski, Wilma Mankiller, Ann Richards, Eleanor Smeal, Condoleezza Rice, Lady Bird Johnson, Coretta Scott King, Madeleine Albright, and Elizabeth Dole are all successful women who have promoted political and social agendas for the American public. Each has excellent public speaking skills, but those skills are complemented by a persona that helps the speaker obtain her goals. Our wish is for every woman to consider how to shape and refine her public persona as a key component of effective speaking.

You will note that we provide many examples throughout the handbook based on the accomplishments of women in the public eye. For example, Elizabeth Dole is cited in several chapters. At one point, we thought we might be giving too many examples from Dole's presence in our political lives. However, Mrs. Dole continues to be in the spotlight. *Parade* magazine reported in 1997 that "with the exception of Gen. Colin Powell, Mrs. Dole enjoys the highest popularity ratings of any public figure among registered Republicans" (p. 4). In early 1999, she stepped down as president of the American Red Cross to run for president of the United States (Freedman, 1999). In November 2002, she won a seat in the Senate as a replacement for retiring Senator Jesse Helms of North Carolina. We should look to Elizabeth Dole as a role model for successful public performance.

Another woman who inspired us to consider the aspects of a woman's public persona is former Secretary of State Madeleine Albright. A 1997 headline in the *Greensboro News & Record* caught our eye: "Albright Adds Substance to Style." In the article, the writer profiled Albright as a charmingly confident political figure who took a message on the road that said, "I'm as good as the guys." The article quoted a number of people who characterized Albright's popularity as a combination of the following: she is a woman, she works hard, she projects a more committed image than her predecessor, she is forceful and dynamic, and she cares. In April 1997, she even outscored President Clinton as the country's favorite public official. Madeleine

Albright is a touchstone for this handbook. Her public persona is a combination of all the controversial issues that are present when a woman steps out into public life and onto the speaking platform. She is confident and forceful (like a man), but she cares (like a woman). When she was secretary of state, the press attended to her clothes and outward presentation, but acknowledged she could handle difficult foreign policy problems (like Cuba and Iraq). Americans acted surprised that a woman could be secretary of state, but they cheered her on at the same time. As the newspaper headline declared, Albright has the style of a woman but the substance of a man, so she seems to pass the test. But, our question is, Why can't a woman just be a woman and enjoy success? Why does she have to act like a man, or be the wife of a public figure, to obtain the approval of her constituents? How should a woman develop her talents and skills knowing that gender is always implicitly present in an audience's judgment of her performance? These are difficult questions, and ones that we do not take enough time to ponder or teach public speakers about. These questions are at the heart of the conversations that provided the impulse to write this handbook.

Elizabeth Dole faces the perennial problems of women in the public eye who are married to famous men.

Intended Readers

Any woman who participates in community life, and the majority of women do, can benefit from this handbook. Most of you are traditional college students who use public speaking in your campus organizations, student government, community forums, and classes. If you are in a business communication class, you may be a business major who intends to shape a career in the corporate world or own your own business. Public speaking will be an integral part of your business life, whether it is speaking in training workshops or giving speeches as a CEO. We also recognize the large numbers of women coming back to school after their children are grown. These "nontraditional" college students have a history of participating in their communities, but may not be polished public speakers. Men also can learn something about women speakers and feminine style from studying this handbook.

No matter what your level of experience is in regard to public speaking, this handbook can help you fine tune the skills you already have, or develop new skills that are necessary for your success. We have assembled the latest research findings about effective public speaking, and we have provided practical application by using real life examples, advice, and experience from a wide range of successful women. Unlike many public speaking books aimed at a popular audience, this is not a book solely about being a better speaker in the corporate world (although we certainly address speaking in the workplace). Rather, we are interested in the wide range of contexts that engage women as public speakers. You will find examples from politics, the corporation, academia, and social life. Our goal is to reach a wide range of women who share in common the need to be excellent public speakers.

Preview of the Chapters

This handbook was designed as a supplement to the most popular public speaking textbooks published by Wadsworth. You should realize that this handbook does not contain all the details of the speech-making process, which is why you need a full-fledged textbook. Rather, our text is designed to focus on women and aspects of gender that create special problems or areas of concern for women speakers. Our text combines research findings and speakers' experiences with prescriptions for how to carry out particular skills.

We begin by setting the stage with the basic elements of public speaking: preparing messages, relating to audiences, and delivering messages are the topics covered in Chapters One through Three. Chapter Four addresses technology as a speaker's tool and how technology relates to the basic components of message preparation, message delivery, and audiences. In addition to standing at a lectern with three-by-five-inch index cards, you are just as likely to find yourself using a lavaliere microphone in front of a video or television camera, or speaking at a video conference. A working knowledge of the gendered aspects of technology is essential for participation in public life. Chapter Five discusses various considerations for speaking in context. Specifically, we will talk about gender issues when speaking on special occasions, participating on panels, and speaking in the workplace. After all the technical details are taken care of, we spend the last chapter in the handbook (Chapter Six) conducting a discussion about you as a woman public speaker. We talk about what it means to be a woman in public who is speaking to an audience. We want you to think about your public persona (which may be different from your identity as a private citizen) because it has such an influence on your public speaking.

We see this handbook as a progression of steps that will help you develop techniques, polish skills, and fully mature as a speaker. It can be used by speakers at all different levels of skill and experience. Because this handbook accompanies both traditional public speaking texts and business communication texts, you can use the two as appropriate for the contexts in which you will be speaking.

Special Features

You might already have noticed some of the special features of this handbook. It is designed as a personal workbook. It is sized to fit in a briefcase, gym bag, or handbag. You can carry it with you on a business trip, to the site of a presentation, or keep it at your desk. You are invited to make notes in the margins and record ideas that will make this a personal reference tool. Each chapter is designed to stand alone. There are assessments, templates, and examples to aid you in developing your skills, and all the examples are from women. (Plenty of good role models out there.) There are also boxes with information that will give you an at-a-glance look at various topics. In the back of the handbook is a Pullout Tools section that contains a speech template, checklists, and a list of sources for further study. And finally, you are invited to record your experiences in the last section of the handbook (Journal Notes), so that you can develop your skills and identity over a period of time. When it is not in your briefcase or backpack, put this handbook right by your dictionary, computer manuals, and other basic reference books on your desk. Use this handbook. That is what it was designed for.

Meet the Authors

Finally, we would like to introduce ourselves, as the authors of this handbook, so that you can get an idea of our perspectives and backgrounds. We are college-educated, professional women, and we frequently speak in public. Throughout the book, we will both share our real-life successes and our mistakes so that you can learn from our many trips to the podium and our experiences with diverse audiences. Because we are both steeped in an academic tradition of public speaking, we are also committed to meeting the challenge presented by many women in the lay public who claim that academic women often fail to take their heads out of the clouds and descend the stairs of the ivory tower to share what they know with others. This handbook is dedicated to bridging academia with the real world so that women at all levels of experience can share together what we know about the many facets of public speaking.

Coauthor Elizabeth ("Jody") Natalle began her public speaking career as the emcee for her fourth-grade talent show at Pinewald Elementary School in 1964. The principal of the school was so impressed with Jody's public speaking that she was invited to serve as emcee for the end-of-the-year awards ceremony for the entire school. Jody never looked back. Her interests in language and culture were cultivated by frequent moves as the daughter of a military family. Jody has a B.A. in foreign language with a second major in communication from the University of Central Florida, and an M.A. and Ph.D. in communication from Florida State University. She taught public speaking at

Pennsylvania State University and now serves as associate professor of communication and women's studies at the University of North Carolina at Greensboro (UNCG), where she has been on the faculty in the Department of Communication for seventeen years. She teaches courses primarily in interpersonal communication, gender studies, and communication theory. She consults regularly on communication topics of interest to business, government, law firms, and hospitals. Her work in the UNCG Women's Studies Program has provided the opportunity for Jody to speak to women in the community and to understand the practical problems involved in shaping public life.

Fritzi Bodenheimer first became interested in public speaking as a member of B'nai B'rith Girls, an international organization for teenagers focused on leadership training and community service. She soon realized that members who gave convincing speeches were elected to the highest offices in the organization. Wasting no time, she wrote her first speech and became local chapter president at the age of fourteen. Fritzi holds a B.S. degree in public relations/mass communication from Boston University and an M.A. in speech communication from UNCG, where she also taught the basic public speaking course. Fritzi lives in Washington, D.C., where she is an assistant professor of public speaking at Montgomery College and an independent communication consultant. She is a cofounder of Women in Training, an organization founded to empower women who train others in a variety of skills, and she is an active member of Women of Washington.

As coauthors and colleagues, we have worked together for thirteen years. In that time we have taught each other about public speaking, computer technology, feminism, and communication theory. Our shared knowledge has made us better at what we do for a living, and we have developed the bonds of friendship along the way. This book is an expression of our professional respect for each other and a gift to other women. We hope you will enjoy *The Woman's Public Speaking Handbook*. Most of all, we hope this book helps you develop the skills that will assist you to go out into the community and articulate an agenda that will make life better for yourself and all those people with whom you have built relationships. The strategic and ethical use of public speaking is truly what characterizes a democracy.

Breakpoint! Think back on your experience as a public speaker. Reflect for awhile to remind yourself about your history and the way it has shaped you to be the speaker you are today. Before you read further, take time to record the following:

First experience as a public speaker: (This might be a good anecdote for future speeches.)

_____

_____

_____

Strengths as a speaker: (Let this book help you fine tune your strengths.)

_____

_____

_____

Weaknesses as a speaker: (Use this book to help you correct or improve weaknesses.)

_____

_____

_____

How might the fact that you are a woman influence you as a public speaker?

_____

_____

_____

CHAPTER ONE

Preparing the Message

Getting Organized

So, you have been asked to make a speech. Whether making a political speech at a community rally or giving a report in class, most people react with a combination of anxiety and excitement when they are asked to speak in public. Susan Faludi, author of the national bestseller *Backlash: The Undeclared War Against Women*, writes that "for the author of what was widely termed an 'angry' and 'forceful' book, I exhibit a timorous verbal demeanor" (1992, p. 10). In preparation for a lecture at the Smithsonian Institution during the book tour, Faludi's publicist tried to rally the reluctant speaker, noting how wonderful it was that so many people wanted to hear her ideas. Faludi replied, "About as wonderful as walking down the street with no clothes on."

If, like Faludi, your first reaction to the prospect of speaking in public is "I'll get butterflies in my stomach and forget everything," you are not alone. And if you think, "I can't possibly get all my points across in ten minutes—I need more time," you are in good company. These reservations are common for both experienced and beginning speakers, whether delivering a formal speech, facilitating a training workshop, or simply introducing another speaker. The first step is to put that nervous energy to good use, and there is no better use than getting organized.

Organization is the key to any good speech. Speakers who deliver dynamic and thought-provoking speeches, seemingly without index cards, notes, or teleprompters, have actually spent many hours preparing, which is exactly why they are able to make such dynamic and thought-provoking speeches. Audiences react more favorably to well-organized speeches because they comprehend them better. So, if you are asking members of your congregation to give fifty dollars to the building fund, they are more likely to respond with a check if your presentation is easy to follow. And organized speakers are perceived as more credible by their audiences; that is, audiences are more likely to believe what the speakers are saying and change their behaviors accordingly.

Getting organized has one more advantage. You will feel less anxious if you are in control—in the driver's seat, so to speak. Instead of driving around lost, the organized speaker has a map, usually in the form of an outline, and knows exactly where she is going.

Your primary textbook is designed to prepare you in all the technical aspects of organizing a speech. You will learn in your text about establishing specific goals within the broader context of informative, persuasive, or special occasion speeches. You will learn about situational variables that influence speech preparation, such as occasion, environment, special audience characteristics, and time of day or year. Your primary text will also offer extensive information about selecting an organizational structure for the speech content and researching supporting material. If you do not have your primary text with you as you are reading this chapter, then go to the Pullout Tools in the back of this handbook. The first tool is a Presentation Checklist. Refresh your memory by studying the first eleven items on the checklist. The second tool is a Speech Outline Template. This tool will help you visualize what the end product will look like. Once you have refreshed your memory, read on about gender considerations when it comes to the technicalities of speech preparation.

What Does Gender Have to Do With It?

Much has been written over the last few years by scholars, such as social psychologist Mary Crawford (1995) and linguist Deborah

Tannen (1990, 1994), about the differences between men's and women's communication styles in conversation. Deborah Tannen tells us that, for women, conversations are a way of establishing and maintaining relationships with others, whether they are speaking with men, women, friends, or coworkers. In contrast, men engage in conversations to demonstrate knowledge and, hence, maintain their social status and independence. In other words, conversation for men is part of an ongoing process that Tannen describes as "oneupmanship" in a world that men see as having a "hierarchical social order" (1990, p. 77). Neither style of communicating is right or wrong, and the male style is not strictly used by men, nor is the female style strictly used by women. For that reason, we will refer hereafter to feminine or masculine styles, noting that men may favor a feminine style, and women a masculine style.

These different styles of communicating in conversation may also play out when speaking in public. In the masculine style of public speaking, the speaker commands respect and attention, and proving or winning points by using "expert" data is favored. Farrell writes that in the rhetorical style that men favor, "the speaker or writer is *for* one thing and *against* another" (1979, p. 916). In contrast, in the feminine style of rhetoric, the speaker emphasizes building a relationship with the audience and favors the use of personal stories to support ideas. Communication expert Patricia Kuchon adds: "I think that in their presentations, women take their audience into account much more than men do. I think they focus on the receivers whereas men are more inclined to talk for themselves—what can they tell people rather than what do people want to hear" (Adubato, 1998, p. 19).

In the masculine style, the speaker usually selects a linear organizational pattern. In other words, the speaker presents the thesis or central premise and then, one by one, discusses the main ideas that support that premise. This style resembles the one Aristotle proposed two thousand years ago—you state your case, and then you prove it. This style, often called the Aristotelian style, or agonistic style, is still commonly used in American debate and platform speaking.

However, a new and "effeminate" style of communicating has emerged in the television age, according to communication scholar Kathleen Hall Jamieson (1988). Her model of "electronic eloquence" is feminine because speech on television is characterized by narrative, visual imagery, and self-disclosure. Jamieson contends that the speaking style presented via television is actually what most Americans prefer. Public speaking teacher Todd Frobish (2000) notes that many public speaking textbooks still focus on the Aristotelian, or masculine, techniques of speech making when we should be teaching students the feminine model offered by Jamieson. If Frobish is correct, then many women have an advantage because they are taught masculine techniques but also know feminine techniques.

For a speaker with a feminine style, the organizational pattern selected is often less direct. The speaker may imply or suggest connections and relationships between points, but will not state them definitively, allowing the audience to draw their own conclusions. The main idea may be stated in the middle of the speech rather than in the beginning. In contrast to the masculine style, which resembles a straight line, the feminine style is more like a web. Suffragette Elizabeth Cady Stanton was one of the first women in America to use a web-like structure to organize her speeches. Her speech entitled "The Solitude of Self" is a good example to study (Tweeten, 1992). Today, the person who carries this style to its limits is feminist theologian Mary Daly (1995). Her speeches not only have a circular and intersecting structure, but she often invents language—for example, "gynenergy," "crone-logical," "snool"—to express her thoughts when ordinary language simply will not do the job.

Communication scholars Karen Foss and Sonja Foss write that gender "functions as the lens through which all other perceptions pass" (1989, p. 67). As women speakers, then, we face a unique challenge in the public speaking situation. Because the masculine style of public speaking and communicating is the dominant one in our society, both men and women are trained in this style. The challenge to a woman public speaker is to present her voice, either feminine or masculine, in a way that is true to her experiences, perceptions, and style, so that the audience does not just hear the speech but carefully listens, contemplating and considering her ideas. The rest of this chapter, and indeed the whole handbook, is about this challenge and how to select strategies to complement your personal style.

A Note on Terminology

Most people know the word *rhetoric* as a negative term meaning hot air, or speech with no meaning. News reporters are quick to talk about "the rhetoric on Capitol Hill" as debate that goes nowhere. Contrary to this public (mis)understanding, the technical term *rhetoric* means persuasion or communication. So, in this handbook, we use rhetorical style to mean persuasive style or communication style.

Other terms that might be confusing to you include *sex* and *gender*. You have probably already noted that *men* and *women, sex* and *gender,* and *masculine* and *feminine* are used in pairs in this handbook. We should clarify these pairs so that you can better see where you fit. Sex differences refer to the biological distinction of males and females, or men and women. Scientific research shows that men and women often behave differently, sometimes as a result of biological causes. But, what happens in our society is that we teach males and females to take on a sex role that goes with what we think a man or a woman should be acting like. These socially constructed and learned roles are the basis for acting masculine or acting feminine. Masculinity and femininity are the internalized mind-set and corresponding outward behaviors that we learn from society, which are really mapped onto our biology. Such internalized psychology and outward feminine or masculine style is what we know as gender. Most people believe that there is a direct correspondence between biology and gender; for example, a female will act feminine. The truth is, gender tends to be more flexible than biology, so that people exhibit gender in different degrees; that is, some people are more masculine (or feminine) than others. We also know that there are exceptions and variations to the patterns: some men act more feminine in style, some women act more masculine in style, and some people can be a combination of masculine and feminine (known as androgynous). Only you know your true gender. In this book, we are working from the premise that many women have internalized and act out a certain amount of feminine behavior. As you read and think about yourself as a woman speaker, you will want to make adjustments to your own style based on your understanding of who you are. Our overall goal is for you to use the information in this book to become more comfortable with your role as a public speaker and put forward a polished style, no matter how feminine or masculine. In fact, we suggest that you experiment with blending feminine and masculine communication characteristics until you arrive at a style that represents you in a credible and professional manner.

As you develop your own style and technique as a public speaker, it is also exciting to think about the way you might contribute to the changing definitions of who is a public speaker and what counts as effective public speaking. Lesley Di Mare offers a challenge that we take seriously: "Aristotle's original statement that rhetoric is the search for all the available means of persuasion in a given situation should be the impetus for society to reconstruct perceptions concerning accepted forms of rhetorical processes, as well as who might utilize those processes and in what contexts. New forms of persuasion must blend with the old so that the rhetorical tradition comes to reflect both masculine and feminine processes" (1992, p. 48). We want you to think about your contributions to public notions of effective speaking. Although we speak about masculine and feminine style, we do not mean to bifurcate or suggest that the two styles are diametrically opposed. There is a range of style to consider, even though the public is still used to the idea that, perhaps, men are stylistically masculine and women are more feminine. You have the potential to be a role model in your own sphere of influence, so we hope you will respond by setting goals that ultimately go beyond your personal development. Share what you have learned with other women and men in your community.

We want to emphasize that inexperienced public speakers may actually be more comfortable learning the linear model of speech organization; that is, introduction, body, conclusion, three main points, and supporting material. Let us take a moment to consider this traditional approach and then talk about an alternative. For a beginning speaker who needs help with the basics, such as a thesis statement and main points, we think you will find the linear approach to be highly useful. And, yes, it is in the traditional masculine style of organizing and thinking. When giving informative speeches, many women who use this masculine style are perfectly comfortable. That is because most people in American culture are taught to organize information in the typical patterns of chronological order, problem and solution, topical main points, and so on. The comfort level changes, however, when the task is to present a persuasive speech. This is when many women are not so comfortable with the traditional methods of problem solving and cause-and-effect reasoning. Speech teacher Taresa Tweeten, who is a colleague of ours, has studied this phenomenon in some depth, including writing a master's thesis on feminine and masculine organizational structures of public speeches (1992). She tells us about her observations in her public speaking courses:

> Many women speakers in my public speaking courses excel in the informative and special occasion speaking portions of the class. They enjoy the opportunity to share topics with others that they perceive as valuable. However, this often changes when we begin to discuss persuasion. For many of my students, persuasion creates apprehension and discomfort. When required to "discover all the available means of persuasion" [a famous phrase from Aristotle's *Rhetoric*] for the purposes of changing audience beliefs, values, or attitudes, some of my students cringe. Only weeks before, the same students demonstrated excellent skills as speakers. When asked about their apprehension, students will offer such responses as, "I don't like pushing my opinions on others" or "persuasion makes me feel uncomfortable."
>
> I have concluded that the primary concern for many of these students is not that they lack confidence or competence, but fear a loss of connection with their audience. This fear of disconnection often leads them to make different choices and even to deviate from traditional advice that I may offer about speech construction. Consequently, the general purpose of their speeches is not necessarily "to persuade my audience to think like me, share my values, or agree with my policy," but instead shifts "to persuade my audience **to listen** to my beliefs, values, and policies, and based upon the connection I am making with you, I want to persuade you to re-examine your own beliefs, values, or policies." The focus of the persuasion seems to be an invitation for dialogue versus an attempt to change attitudes, beliefs, or behaviors.
>
> This attempt to indirectly persuade sets up an interesting, nondefensive, but arousing dynamic with the audience. It is almost as if the speaker uses the event to ready the audience for the possibility of future change rather than immediate change. Throughout the speech, connection (common ground) is often stressed more than or equally to differences of opinion. The speaker goes to great lengths to create a speech that seeks to connect with the audience on several levels. In researching supporting material, the speaker will seek common ground in looking for evidence. The organizational structure is often indirect. Content often returns to common

threads of agreement between speaker and audience. Thus, the speaker often uses a nonlinear or configural pattern of organization rather than the traditional linear rhetorical structure.

The student arrives at this approach because she *feels* this is the best way to accomplish her goals as a speaker. These "unorthodox" methods produce highly effective speeches. They tend to be much more interpersonal in nature and create a positive communication climate. As more and more speakers find success using such an alternative approach, it opens the door for society to accept the validity of these methods. (Tweeten, 1997)

Professor Tweeten's observations are worth noting here. We want you to organize your speech in a manner that is logically consistent with your ability to put ideas together. Two communication scholars who agree with Tweeten's experience are Sonja Foss and Karen Foss. They have written a textbook entitled *Inviting Transformation: Presentational Speaking for a Changing World* (2003). In this book, you can read about the dialogic approach to public speaking. Sonja Foss and Cindy Griffin (1995) have developed a more extended feminist theory of rhetoric that is based on the concept of inviting speakers and audience members to share points of view rather than having a speaker try to convert an audience to an intended position on an issue. Invitational rhetoric, as Foss and Griffin named their theory, contends that sharing viewpoints leads to understanding as a necessary step before someone chooses to change his or her mind. This view is quite a departure from traditional views on persuasion, but it helps to explain why students like Professor Tweeten's feel better about locating points of agreement with their audience than using direct persuasion.

One of the main characteristics of feminine style is structuring a speech around a narrative, or storytelling. An excellent example of a speech structured around a narrative is by Karen Stephenson (1992), a professor of anthropology at UCLA. In her speech, entitled "How to Lead People" and published in *Vital Speeches of the Day*, Professor Stephenson used her observations as an anthropologist to inspire the entering MBA class at orientation. After an introduction using the hypothetical example of a tribal chief in an American corporate boardroom, she tells three successive stories to illustrate the way culture constrains business practices. The stories are emotional and grab the listener. As the speech comes to a close, Stephenson advocates that all MBA students take advantage of the new emphasis on business ethics to change institutional practices. The speech is one you may wish to study as an alternative approach to organizing your own speeches.

Another resource that you may find helpful is the chapter on narrative in Clella Jaffe's textbook entitled *Public Speaking: A Cultural Perspective* (2001). In this chapter, Professor Jaffe discusses the rich heritage behind the use of narratives, or stories, as both the subject matter and the form for organizing speeches. She points out that Native Americans are excellent role models as speakers because they often use narrative to explain, persuade, and model behavior for others. In addition, two narrative organizational patterns are discussed: the infinity loop, where a theme is developed through a series of stories, and the exemplum, where the speaker uses a combination of a quotation and follow-up stories to relate a theme to the audience.

Speech preparation may seem overwhelming at first. But, as we said in the beginning of this chapter, it all starts with your specific goal. When you are speaking about a topic you know well and feel strongly or even passionately about, the rest will follow easily.

CHAPTER TWO

Relating to the Audience

Audiences come in all sizes and are composed of a wide range of people. An old rule in teaching public speaking is to tell the speaker to do an audience analysis. Advertisers do the same thing, but call it market analysis. In today's sophisticated world, researching facts about an audience includes demographics (sex, age, occupation, political party affiliation, income, and so on) and psychographics (attitudes about topics or issues you are likely to be speaking about). You must do audience analysis at some level if you are going to connect with the people who will be listening to you. Like an advertiser, you are usually selling something—a product, an idea, a service, or yourself. It pays to take the time to do the audience analysis (as any good advertiser will tell you). In this chapter, we are going to cover four aspects of audiences that have links to gender: researching an audience, preparing for and meeting a hostile audience, working an audience, and working with an audience over a period of time.

Researching an Audience

Basic audience analysis involves finding out as much as possible about the audience you will be addressing. If you receive an invitation to speak, ask questions pertinent to what you will be talking about so you can get your bearings. A simple checklist can become a mental habit after a time. If you are unfamiliar with audience analysis, use the following questions to get started.

    _____ How many people will be in attendance?

    _____ Are they male or female? Proportion of male to female?

    _____ What is the age range?

    _____ What is the racial or ethnic makeup of the audience?

    _____ What is the socioeconomic status of the group in general?

    _____ What is the level of education or preparedness for this topic?

    _____ What is the predominant religious affiliation of this audience?

    _____ Is this a professional group or a lay audience?

    _____ What attitudes toward the speaker or topic is the audience likely to have?

    _____ How will the audience be seated during the event?

    _____ What other aspects of the physical environment may affect the audience?

    _____ Where is my speech in the sequence of events?

    _____ How will the occasion affect the mind-set of the audience?

    _____ What political party do the majority of audience members belong to?

    _____ What stories will appeal to the audience? How can we connect?

Notice that this checklist is full of implications for diversity. Audiences are not monolithic or homogeneous. Rather, audiences run the gamut when it comes to race, class, gender, sexual orientation, geographic location, and so on. Such diversity of background affects the way you approach an audience with a message and the way an audience perceives you as a speaker. You must be aware of this state of affairs, or you will not be successful when it comes to achieving the goals of your speech.

Initial information gathered by asking questions will immediately provide you with some boundaries and direction in selecting examples and language for your speech. Audience analysis also allows you to reflect on what the audience might expect from you as a speaker. For example, if you are an African American woman, would a predominantly African American audience be expecting to connect with you on a level that might be different from a predominantly Caucasian audience or a mixed-race audience?

Thinking through the attitudes and expectations of an audience not only allows you to reflect on the audience's perception of you, but forces you to confront expectations and stereotypes you may have about the audience. Do you think all lawyers are argumentative and out to get you on the issue? Are older audiences more hostile about the role of women in the public eye? After careful reflection, you may decide that your own preconceived notions about your audience are not quite right. Keep an open mind so that you don't miss pertinent information beforehand that will help ensure a successful speech rather than one that insults or condescends

Traditional Audience Analysis

Professor Natalle has spoken on several occasions to a literary society whose members meet at the Greensboro Country Club. This organization

---

THE MYTH OF WOMEN'S PERSUASIBILITY

When researchers first started looking scientifically at audience characteristics back in the 1950s, sex differences were viewed as part of personality. Women were deemed more persuadable than men. We now know that conclusion to be a common stereotype that reads "women are more gullible than men." After an analysis of virtually all of the persuasion research available from the 1930s to the late 1980s, communication researchers Kimber Charles Pearce and Elizabeth Natalle concluded that there is no discernible or real scientific connection between sex differences or gender and persuasibility. The common belief that women are more easily persuaded than men is unfounded. This new information liberates a public speaker to make better choices based on solid audience analysis rather than stereotyped beliefs.

(Source: Kimber Charles Pearce & Elizabeth J. Natalle. (1993). Deconstructing Gender Differences in Persuasibility: A Bricolage. *Women's Studies in Communication, 16,* 55–73.)

is all female, almost exclusively Caucasian, college educated, more Republican than Democrat, and well read on a range of literary topics. There are several mother-and-daughter pairs in the membership, and the age range is from approximately forty to eighty. The club meets once a month for a sit-down lunch at Greensboro's oldest and most exclusive country club. A speaker addresses the group after the meal, usually on a timely topic with some literary connection. The speech runs for about twenty minutes with a ten-minute question-and-answer period. I initially gathered audience information by asking the program chair, who invited me to speak, to tell me a little bit about the membership. I later saw a membership roster that gave me the names of many prominent community women whose names appear often in the local press. By keeping a sharp eye on this group, I have added bits of information over time to get to know this audience even better and what they expect in a speaker.

On my latest speaking engagement to the literary society, I spoke to them (at their request) about popular books on the market regarding gender and communication styles. In addition to taking a stand on the merits of the selected bestsellers discussed, my audience analysis told me to spice up the talk with anecdotes about married life that would connect to this audience. During the question-and-answer period (Q & A), I fielded an inquiry about gender and communication issues relevant to the O. J. Simpson trial. This was not totally unexpected given the number of attorneys I knew to be present in the audience, and the discussion added a new dimension to the topic at hand. The speech was well received, in large part, because the audience analysis revealed ways for me to make the speech more relevant to the characteristics of the audience.

In fact, being invited to speak at lunch or dinner is often the easiest type of speaking engagement. A conversation over a meal is a good way to build rapport with some of your audience members before the speech begins. In addition, by getting to know your audience, your nervousness often starts to diminish and you may even begin to enjoy the conversation. Keep in mind, however, that your most important job is to deliver an effective speech. You may need to politely excuse yourself to conduct a final check on equipment, review your notes, or refresh yourself. These few moments away from the table can make a big difference in the end.

There are, however, many other types of speaking situations that require more in-depth audience analysis. For example, all of the following speaking assignments need both demographic and psychographic information about the audience: training, selling a product, political campaigning, arguing a community issue before a board, fundraising, and convention keynoting. In these situations, a speaker must rely on contacts and other sources of information to compose a profile of the audience and determine how they will respond to all aspects of the message.

In 1992, Professor Natalle had an opportunity to serve as a convention keynote speaker at the North Carolina Bar Association. My topic was gender and communication in the legal profession. I had about six months of lead time before the convention, and I used that time to get to know attorneys, judges, and law professors in a way that I had not previously known them. I made telephone calls to attorneys that I knew or whose names had been given to me to get to know their views on the topic of my speech. I sent a list of questions to several attorneys I knew very well to get a set of examples. I went to dinner with several attorneys, judges, and law professors to chat over a meal about the membership of the Bar and how they would view the topic. And, of course, I conducted library research and perused legal documents to compose speech content that would appeal to this audience. This process was time consuming and involved in-depth investigation, but it paid off on the day I delivered the keynote. The speech went so well that I received invitations to speak, conduct workshops, and consult with law firms for the next two years.

An interesting and effective example of good audience analysis can be found in a 1982 speech given by Geraldine Ferraro at the annual meeting of the National Association of Women Judges. At the time, Ms. Ferraro was a member of the U.S. House of Representatives from New York, and the meeting she keynoted was held in New York City. Her speech, entitled "Who Will Fight for the Worth of Women's Work?," was organized as a forensic argument and opened with the following setup: "But I am here to plead a case. My case is that women in leadership positions make a real difference in the way our society works. And I believe that women like us must continue to make that difference" (p. 70). Ferraro proceeded to succinctly persuade her female audience that they should take a lead in making and interpreting laws that would ensure fairness to working women as a means to improve the lives of all citizens. Ferraro capitalized on the mind-set and judicial perspective of the audience by organizing the speech as a reasoned, legal argument and persuading through appropriate appeals such as statistics, reference to legal cases, comparison, and first person examples. She not only set out the facts regarding issues such as comparable worth and women in poverty, but flattered the audience by showing her appreciation for their intelligence and role in society. The speech cleverly ends with the entreaty: "Madam Justices, I rest my case. The verdict is yours" (p. 73). This speech is one that I keep in my files and frequently refer to as a "well-made speech" because it is so tightly constructed with total consideration for the intended audience.

Nontraditional Audience Analysis

Martha Solomon Watson is an expert on public speakers who have participated in the American women's movement. Professor Watson (1995, 1999) has studied Anna Howard Shaw, Emma Goldman, Mary Church Terrell, Elizabeth Cady Stanton, Frances Willard, and Phyllis Schlafly, to name just a few. What Watson has discovered is that, outside the realm of political or forensic argument such as the Ferraro speech described above, many women speakers tell stories as a basis for their speeches. Through storytelling, rather than formal reasoned argument, speakers and audiences come together to make meaning out of the rhetorical situation at hand. In other words, Watson says, we tell stories as the basis for public discourse, and the audience participates in developing meaning by connecting to the story. If this theory is correct, we have an important lesson to learn from Watson's study of American speakers: the intent of the speaker may not be as important as we think it is when it comes to assessing the effects of a speaking situation. Why is this so? Watson claims that ordinary people often do not hear the rational argument or formal reasoning in public speech; rather, the audience listens for a story line that allows for a connection of familiarity. When the connection is made, meaning is generated and the audience is moved. Each individual in the audience is moved in a slightly different way and arrives at a personalized form of "the truth." Importantly, the kind of story that an audience often identifies with is autobiography. When a speaker stands before an audience and says, "Let me tell you my story," the audience members prick up their ears and get ready to hear the human side of the issue.

AIDS activist Mary Fisher uses her personal story about living with AIDS to ask audiences to "embrace moral courage." Fisher spoke at the 1996 Republican National Convention, and as the camera panned the audience, one could see people crying as a result of hearing her story. Each person connected to Fisher's story in a personalized way. Embracing moral courage meant something different to each who participated in hearing her story. (In a subsequent section of this chapter [Preparing for a Hostile Audience], note how Fisher is described as a speaker who reduces negative emotion regarding a controversial topic like AIDS through the device of her autobiography.)

At a 1996 campaign rally in North Carolina, Elizabeth Dole used her husband's autobiography as a way to move voters into identifying with Bob Dole's character as something worthy of the presidency. As Elizabeth Dole related the story of her husband, the audience's attention was riveted on her, even though they had heard about Bob Dole's poor farm family and military service many times before. The telling of that story personalized the candidate's qualifications for president, and it did not hurt that the storyteller was a native North Carolinian whom many audience members identified with as the local girl from down the road in Salisbury. Just as important, Elizabeth Dole was synonymous with her husband because the story and the storyteller merged as the story was told over and over throughout Elizabeth Dole's many campaign stops in the fall of 1996. Note also that Dole's speech was structured in three parts: the story of Bob Dole, his vision of America, and his record in Congress. The autobiography hooked the audience members before they had to undertake the more difficult task of listening to a description of his vision and service record.

Do women like you tell stories? Of course. In 1996, Professor Natalle attended a conference sponsored by North Carolina (NC)

Equity, the agency that lobbies the state legislature regarding issues for women and children. The leadership director of NC Equity, Jackie McKinnon, was the sixth speaker in the morning lineup (a difficult position to be in as a speaker, because the audience is growing restless and needs a break at that point). As she began to tell us about how the women of North Carolina were participating in establishing the 1996–97 legislative agenda (which was the purpose of her speech), she told her own personal story about how she came to NC Equity. Her story about herself as a single mother with little in the way of resources was told with such conviction and sincerity that the audience tuned in to every word she said. She made us feel the importance of the work of NC Equity by telling how this agency not only helped her out of a tough time, but it had become the vehicle through which women could help other women in a statewide effort. At the close of her speech, about one hundred people were ready to burst out of that auditorium and get down to the business of voting on the most important issues that North Carolina would need to attend to during the upcoming legislative session to improve the lives of women and children.

We would like to suggest that analyzing an audience by determining the appropriateness of the story you have to tell may be an extremely effective way to reach an audience. Our caution is that you

---

Homework Assignment: Studying Women's Speeches

Joy Ritchie and Kate Ronald have edited a collection of speeches and writings by sixty-seven women called *Available Means: An Anthology of Women's Rhetoric(s)*. Speakers include Sojourner Truth, Susan B. Anthony, Toni Morrison, Gloria Anzaldua, and Ruth Bader Ginsburg. This anthology presents a wonderful opportunity for you to study actual speeches, biographical information, and audience response. In reading this anthology, we were struck by the way in which the editors included a variety of approaches to "asserting the right to speak" as a way to teach us that the available means of persuasion do not conform to Aristotle's notions of communication when we consider the history and circumstances of women on the public platform.

(Source: Joy Ritchie & Kate Ronald (2001). *Available Means: An Anthology of Women's Rhetoric(s)*. Pittsburgh: University of Pittsburgh Press.)

select the story as a form of speaking because it is the best way for you to express yourself and address the topic of your speech. The sincerity of personal experience should be just that—sincere rather than contrived—or an audience will detect that they are being manipulated.

Occasion and Audience Mind-Set

The occasion itself has a way of affecting the mind-set of the audience. Celebrations elicit a highly charged positive energy and an audience ready to accept your words and celebrate with you. Solemn occasions, something very formal or religious in nature, elicit a quiet calm among audience members who are usually prepared to reflect thoughtfully on your words and engage in ritualized or rule-oriented behavior. For example, First Lady Laura Bush was highly praised for her ability to gauge the mind-set of the American public after the World Trade Center bombing when she traveled around the country to mourn with grieving families (Gerhart, 2001). As a speaker, your job is to honor the occasion and the expectations of the audience.

The following example further illustrates the mind-set of the audience. In 1997, retired Congresswoman Shirley Chisholm visited UNCG as the featured speaker at the annual Martin Luther King, Jr. Celebration. The occasion was clearly a happy one and served as the culmination of Black History Month activities on campus. The largely student audience came to enjoy themselves, to celebrate the end of a month's worth of hard work implementing all the activities, and to honor the celebrity of Ms. Chisholm and the memory of Dr. King. The audience was primarily young and African American, so a sense of high energy and solidarity was also present. Shirley Chisholm had no problem tuning in to the mind-set of this audience and working her magic as a speaker. Although she looked like a benevolent grandmother, when it was time for her to ascend the stage, she jumped up the steps in high heels and got her speech underway at a brisk pace. She kept up with these young people and bolstered the energy level with her exhortations to the students to take charge of the social problems facing America and to give back to the black community. The students loved her, and Ms. Chisholm proved highly successful as a speaker who honored both the occasion and the expectations of the audience.

Preparing For a Hostile Audience

Hostile audiences are as much a reality today as they were two hundred years ago. An instructive history lesson takes us back to May 17, 1838, when a wild mob of Philadelphians burned down Pennsylvania Hall in reaction to the presence of Angelina Grimké as a speaker at an abolitionist society meeting (Campbell, 1989). Ms. Grimké is better known as the woman who broke the barrier against women speaking in public in the United States than she is for the effect she had on the anti-slavery movement. Unfortunately, the extremity of the situation in Philadelphia put an end to her public speaking career, but Angelina Grimké's experience is one that has been repeated in lesser degrees over the centuries and serves as a potent reminder that hostility, at its worst, can be life threatening. At the least, a hostile audience can disrupt delivery and compromise the effect of a message. Sexism and racism are still alive, and women of all colors need to be aware of this before stepping onto the public platform.

THE ARGUMENT CULTURE

Deborah Tannen's book *The Argument Culture* establishes the premise that we live in a world where everyone wants to argue or debate rather than engage in dialogue as a matter of communication. She says, "In the argument culture, criticism, attack, or opposition are the predominant if not the only ways of responding to people or ideas" (p. 7). This is one explanation for the degree of hostility that public speakers may encounter. We encourage you to read and reflect on Professor Tannen's book.

(Source: Deborah Tannen. (1998). *The Argument Culture: Moving From Debate to Dialogue*. New York: Random House.)

There are often situations where the speaker knows in advance that the audience may be hostile to her presence, her message, or both. In strategically planning to meet such an audience, there are several general principles to keep in mind.

First, women are still generally viewed as less credible speakers than men just by the mere fact that the speaker is female. Some interesting research by psychologist Patricia Conner-Greene (1996) confirms that women are perceived as less persuasive, confident, intelligent, knowledgeable, and competent than men; yet audiences are equally persuaded by female and male speakers in actuality. What this means is that an audience may be persuaded by a female speaker, but that same audience may not give the speaker credit for effecting the attitude change. So, the good news is that women are equal to men in achieving persuasion; they just will not be acknowledged for it. The bad news is that a woman has a strike against her each time she steps on the stage to speak, and so must "work" the audience that much more than a man, or at least work it differently than a man.

Sexism joined forces with hostility during a 1998 Massachusetts election. Jane Swift was running for lieutenant governor and just happened to be pregnant during the campaign. Ellen Goodman wrote a column for *The Boston Globe* in which she described the remarks that Swift received everywhere she campaigned. The comments ranged from "she should quit" to "she's being selfish" to "if she wasn't planning to stay home, she'd be better off having a cat." Rather than concentrating on campaign issues, Jane Swift had to endure the hostility of peers and citizens who seemed to think that women who bear children cannot run for public office.

The second general principle to keep in mind when preparing to meet a hostile audience is that the speaker cannot expect to turn an audience around 180 degrees. Human nature just isn't like that. A realistic expectation is that you move an audience a little further in the direction of the desired change, and leave the door open for further persuasion. For example, most people want the medical community to find a cure for AIDS, yet both ordinary citizens and government have not backed the research effort when the effort is measured by the amount of funding targeted for AIDS research. Why? Audiences are naturally hostile to this appeal because, in the audience's collective mind, AIDS is seen as a gay problem or a drug addict problem. Mary Fisher, the AIDS activist mentioned earlier in this chapter, became a high profile speaker after two emotional appearances at the Republican National Conventions of 1992 and 1996. Although her audiences often come into a room with a hostile, antigay, antidrug mind-set, she is able to use her excellent abilities as an emotional speaker to move the audience in the short run. Her conversational style, perfect pacing, sincere vocal expression, as well her own story, serve as an emotional catch to bring her audiences to tears. Whether or not Fisher has made much impact on

AIDS as a topic for our national agenda or in the funding of AIDS research by Republican sources, she has learned to use public speaking skills to open the door for further persuasion.

The third principle to remember is that a speaker meeting a hostile audience must be prepared for the boomerang effect. A classic theory in the persuasion literature, put forth by Carl Hovland and his associates in the 1950s (Hovland, Janis, & Kelley, 1953), says that sometimes a hostile audience will be so disenchanted with a speaker's attempt at persuasion that the audience's attitude will boomerang, or move in the opposite direction of the position recommended. Ralph Rosnow and Edward Robinson (1967) summarized triggers of the boomerang effect thirty years ago, but they still seem relevant today. A boomerang effect might occur because a speaker's argument is poorly constructed. Or, the message itself might cause aggression and extreme emotional response. Finally, the topic and arguments might make the audience member aware of his or her own counter beliefs. Although it is often difficult to predict exactly what will set off the boomerang effect, it is a real liability when it occurs and one that is difficult to recover from.

In a sense, we think Hillary Rodham Clinton suffered from the boomerang effect in regard to the Whitewater case and her subsequent unpopularity with the American people when she served as first lady. Mrs. Clinton's ratings in national polls continued to decrease as the Whitewater case endured. We think Mrs. Clinton's high profile in this complex case, involving real estate investments and her former law firm, may have touched off an extreme emotional response in many Americans regarding their beliefs about what the first lady should be involved in. The negative press surrounding her involvement in Whitewater set up a hostile climate that was present in many contexts where the first lady needed to meet the public. Her job as a public speaker was made that much more difficult because of this boomerang effect and may even have influenced her effectiveness as an advocate on social issues, particularly the role of women in politics.

As Mrs. Clinton approached her fiftieth birthday, *The New York Times* reported (Broder, 1997) that her aides used the occasion to stage a "reborn" public persona, which de-emphasized previous perceptions of her as a copresident or policy wonk. And, as might be expected,

when President Clinton admitted to inappropriate behavior with Monica Lewinsky, a *CBS Evening News* poll reported in August of 1998 indicated that Americans were two to one in support of Mrs. Clinton. In a Pew Research Center survey, also taken in August of 1998 ("First Lady," 1998), Mrs. Clinton's favorable rating had come from 42 percent back in January of 1996 to 66 percent after her husband's public admission of the relationship with Lewinsky. It took a gender stereotyped situation to reverse what appeared to be a boomerang effect for Hillary Clinton. Even more astonishing, the December 1998 annual Gallup Poll indicated that President Clinton was the most admired man in the United States (even as the U.S. House of Representatives had just impeached him), while First Lady Hillary Clinton garnered the top spot for most admired woman ("Poll Respondents," 1999). Clearly, the public came around. Mrs. Clinton was elected senator from New York in the 2000 elections. This makes for an interesting, and challenging, set of circumstances when it comes to speech preparation.

Meeting the Hostile Audience

Keeping the above commonsense principles in mind, how do you actually meet a hostile audience? Certainly, one way is to be prepared with arguments on both sides of the issue. A second strategy is to take your preparation one step further and open your mind to a multivalued orientation on the topic. An issue usually has more than two sides, so a right versus wrong mentality only sets the speaker and audience up for polarized interaction. Creative solutions to problems need to be found, at times, through dialogue, not monologue. For example, teenage pregnancy is a national problem that polarizes many Americans. The perception is that teenagers are purposely getting pregnant as a means to qualify for welfare aid. Cutting teenagers off from welfare is probably not the only solution, or appropriate resolution, to this complex social problem. Taxpayers need to hear about multiple causes and creative solutions for attacking the problem. Faye Wattleton, president of Planned Parenthood from 1978 to 1991, was highly skilled at quelling hostility by bringing audiences around to prevention rather than punishment. In her autobiography, entitled *Life on the Line* (1996), Wattleton makes it known that she treated virtually every audience she spoke to as hostile because not only did she face dissension from much of the public, but there was disagreement inside Planned Parenthood regarding tactics for approaching the controversial topic of reproductive rights for the most persuasive effect.

Wattleton's standard speech on reproductive freedom (Wattleton, 1991, 1994) is a good example of how to take an explosive topic and diffuse it rhetorically. Wattleton used family examples that audience members could relate to ("My daughter Felicia and I have always been open"); she showed how government policies, in spite of good intentions, often lead to negative consequences for a variety of citizens; and she personalized the problem by challenging people to take action based on the circumstances of their own communities and families ("Make sure that your school board . . ."). By transferring responsibility from federal government to the local citizenry, Wattleton's audience was able to see how every community could participate in problem solving. Indeed, Wattleton's position as president of Planned Parenthood required that she develop creativity as a speaker who frequently encountered a hostile public. We think Wattleton did a remarkable job, especially when you consider that she often characterized her own public speaking and advocacy as "going into battle."

Another strategy is to predict the kinds of emotional reactions that are likely to emerge in the speaking situation. Hostility is often accompanied by fear, anger, hate, or other strong emotions. As a speaker, one needs to be prepared to stay cool in the presence of hot tempers. Ask Geraldine Ferraro, who had to debate George H. Bush in 1984 during the vice presidential race. Her request to Bush not to patronize her during an emotional portion of the debate only heightened the negativity felt by many audience members and viewers who were hostile toward a woman candidate from the beginning of the debate. The fact is that most Americans remember the emotional dimension of the Bush-Ferraro debate rather than the content of the debate. This is not a pleasant way to be remembered in the history books.

A good case study of a woman who successfully navigates hostile audiences is Patricia Ireland, former president of the National Organization for Women (NOW). In an interview in *Mother Jones*, Ms. Ireland was asked by interviewer Richard Blow if her presidency "reinforced the perception, right or wrong, that NOW doesn't speak to most women, especially those raising traditional families." Ireland responded, in part, "but most women probably can't identify with someone who's a public speaker and president of NOW anyway" (1996, p. 71). Ireland was aware that the mention of NOW brings up hostility in people, and she was also aware that her own sexuality was an issue that the media continued to focus on to the exclusion of some of the issues that NOW regards as important to American women. Yet, on the public platform, Professor Bodenheimer has observed Patricia Ireland to be a warm, humorous speaker who disarms her audience with sincerity, intelligence, and good presentation skills. One of the lessons to learn from this case study is that hostility may precede you because the media has created a picture of you that is larger than life. A successful public speaker will confront that hyperbole by showing her true self to the extent possible. Patricia Ireland confronted the controversy with grace and dignity every day she served as NOW president.

Taking the above discussion down to a local level, the former mayor of Greensboro, North Carolina, is Carolyn Allen, a woman who has been characterized in the local media as a "tree hugging environmentalist." Dr. Allen and her husband are avid birdwatchers, a pastime that was parlayed into a reputation that resulted in a certain amount of snickering and, yes, hostility, when it came to the public's view of Allen on environmental issues, zoning decisions, and other urban policy debates. In spite of this "granola" characterization, Mayor Allen showed herself to be an intelligent and thoughtful leader who easily won three terms of office. Once again, a woman on the public platform may need to diffuse hostility by counteracting a media image that does not match the person.

Working an Audience

As you become more experienced in your role as a public speaker, you will find yourself developing skills beyond speech preparation and delivery. Getting the most out of a speaking situation for both speaker and audience usually involves learning how to "work an audience." By this phrase we mean learning how to develop a relationship with the audience by creating rapport, creating interaction, and handling question-and-answer sessions. Let's look at each of these skills from a gendered perspective.

To create rapport means to build a bond between speaker and audience. Rapport implies harmony, positivity, and understanding. A speaker can create rapport in a variety of ways. If possible, work with the meeting coordinators to eliminate physical barriers between you and the audience. Reduction of the physical space between audience and speaker can help to create a welcoming environment. Come early enough so that when audience members arrive you can greet them. Several years ago, Professor Bodenheimer attended a series of lectures at the Smithsonian Institution that included many notable speakers. One of the speakers came out from behind the lectern and shook as many hands as possible while people were finding their seats. Of course, this is the speaker I remember. This type of gesture, along with a smile and eye contact, starts to build a bond between the audience and speaker.

Using the research from the audience analysis, make reference to the occasion, a local event or custom, or the geographic area. Showing the audience you have taken the time to get know to them builds good will. The introduction is an appropriate spot for such remarks as evidenced in this speech by Joan Konner (1990), delivered in Paterson, New Jersey. Konner was the dean of the prestigious Columbia University School of Journalism at the time of the speech, and her audience was the New Jersey Press Women's Association. "Good Afternoon. Thank you very much for inviting me. I am pleased to have the chance to address the New Jersey Press Women's Association for several reasons. One, I grew up in New Jersey. Paterson is my hometown. My children and grandchildren still live here. My first job was on the Bergen *Record* . . ." (p. 726).

Breakpoint! Think for a moment about your own techniques or attempts to establish rapport with audiences. Record your successful techniques and set some additional goals if necessary.

Successful techniques to create rapport:

_____

_____

_____

Goals for accomplishing increased rapport:

_____

_____

To build rapport, a speaker must also think about her physical presence. The fact that you are a woman and that you appear feminine (or masculine or androgynous) in your self-presentation is the first bit of information that an audience member uses to decide if he or she will listen. Speakers who meet audience expectations regarding physical presence are likely to move the bonding process forward before ever arriving at the lectern. Society has a bias toward attractive women who dress in a feminine style (Sigelman, Sigelman, & Fowler, 1987). Although we encourage you to develop a personal presentation of self that is consistent with your values, we must note the overwhelming positive reactions of female and male audience members to well-groomed, stylish, attractive speakers. We are not suggesting that every woman on the public platform needs to be attractive, but we are suggesting that a speaker's appearance and voice are regarded by the public as important influences on the ability of the speaker to create and maintain a bond with the audience. Look sharp and use your positive physical attributes as assets to your public speaking.

Jacqueline Kennedy won over America with her personal appearance and elegant manner, which was so strongly positive that audiences easily overlooked her girlish and weak speaking voice (Natalle, in press). Mrs. Kennedy has had a long-lasting influence over what we expect not only from first ladies, but from any woman in the public spotlight. Caroline Kennedy Schlossberg continues that tradition in her rare public speeches, such as the address she gave at the 2000 Democratic National Convention (Schlossberg, 2000). Her reputation as a legal scholar, her renown as a member of the Kennedy family, and her "Kennedy Style" clothing (white A-line dress with double strand pearls) drew a standing ovation before she even uttered her first word. Her measured, confident speaking drew a second standing ovation at the end of her speech.

A public figure who emerged as a favorite role model in the 1990s was former Secretary of State Madeleine Albright. Her style and elegance were evident in her choice of clothes and accessories, a fact that did not go unnoticed by popular women's magazines, as evidenced in the accompanying cartoon.

"Madeleine Albright kicked butt in that suit."

Professor Natalle attended Elizabeth Dole's first speaking engagement after the 1996 Republican National Convention where her husband received the presidential nomination. Mrs. Dole returned to her home state of North Carolina to campaign for her husband and received a resounding welcome at her first stop in Greensboro. I heard audience members all around me whispering to each other, "Isn't she pretty?" Mrs. Dole's attire (an electric blue silk suit, coiffed hair, and polished red fingernails) met this particular audience's expectations. By the time she took center stage, she had already created the necessary rapport to be able to work the audience for maximum response. Unlike Mrs. Kennedy, Mrs. Dole has a strong speaking voice that exudes confidence, and she increased her rapport by adding voice to physical appearance. Speaking of sheer vocal power, Harvard law professor Lani Gaunier and civil rights activist Myrlie Evers-Williams have two of the most powerful voices we have heard. The resonance of their voices draws an audience right in and makes a person want to listen.

THE POWER OF CHARM

What do Jacqueline Kennedy, Johnnetta Cole, Camille Cosby, Elizabeth Dole, and Madeleine Albright have in common? Each woman could be described as charming. *Elle* magazine ran an article protesting uncivil behavior in women today and offered, instead, the notion of charm: "Charm has the power to win over others, boost self-confidence, positively influence society, and foster an allure that can captivate a roomful of people" (p. 302). This point of view suggests that charm is an asset to women on the public platform. Perhaps we should rethink the notion that being charming is old-fashioned. The article in *Elle* defined charm as being authentic, well-mannered, thoughtful of others, and physically poised. How would you define charming?

(Source: Nancy Serano. (2001, March). Charmed, I'm Sure. *Elle*, 302–303.)

Two other examples of the impact of voice and physical appearance come to mind. Jean Kilbourne, the professor who authored *Killing Us Softly* and *Still Killing Us Softly*, which are videotapes about sexist advertising practices, is popular on the college lecture circuit. Her message is delivered via a graphic slide presentation that has a strong feminist message concerning the objectification of the physical body as a means to sell products. She attempts to persuade college audiences not to buy products advertised in such demeaning ways, and she also tries to educate young adults about how heterosexual relationships could be improved if we learned lessons from alternate media messages. Kilbourne's slide lecture is challenging and could be interpreted as controversial; however, she uses well-chosen language to connect to her audience. Professor Natalle attended one of Kilbourne's lectures in 1996. In a darkened hall, Kilbourne reeled the audience in as she confidently and intelligently spoke about her topic. Her face was lighted by the lectern—an attractive face (which presents a certain irony given her topic) that also was the source of a strong voice speaking out in the dark as slide after slide brought the message home (Kilbourne, 1996). She held five hundred audience members captive for forty-five minutes. Talk about rapport!

At the opposite end of the continuum, Professor Natalle once saw antipornography activist Andrea Dworkin (1985) deliver a slide lecture that failed to capture the audience because of her problematic vocal delivery. As Dworkin began her lecture, she developed an alarming pattern of gasping for air as she spoke. I was so concerned that she was on the verge of a heart attack or asthma attack, that I had difficulty connecting her powerful words with the riveting slides.

Another technique to work an audience involves creating interaction. In this handbook, we stress a conversational style of speaking as an effective way to speak and gain response from the audience. Working an audience is not a Machiavellian concept. Although you have goals as a speaker, ethical principles stipulate that you work with, rather than manipulate, an audience to achieve desired effects. Your ability to create interaction may be affected by your place in the sequence of events for the occasion. If you are the featured speaker, then you are the entire focus, and the audience can concentrate its energy on what you may be asking it to do. If, however, you are the third or fourth speaker, or the last speaker before a break, then your job of creating and sustaining interaction will be more difficult. You will want to watch the feedback your audience is giving and make adjustments as necessary. You may even find yourself cutting parts of your speech if you sense the audience cannot stay with you. But, let's focus on the positive and assume ideal conditions for the discussion that follows.

Creating interaction can happen on two levels: overt audience participation or internal thinking and response in audience members' minds. Let's talk about audience participation first. A lot of speech trainers mistakenly advocate that all public speeches should begin with a joke to engage audience participation. Telling a good joke takes a certain amount of skill, and many people simply are not good at joke telling. Telling a joke in a speech just because you feel obligated is the quickest way to ensure disaster. If a joke bombs in the introduction, then the audience's expectations are lowered regarding the credibility and capability of the speaker. Bad jokes, inappropriate jokes, or unsuccessful humor leave the audience flat, and put the speaker in the awkward position of having to recover. There is also some evidence from humor expert Regina Barreca (1991) that women are not as adept at joking as men because women do not grow up developing joking skills like men do. If you know you are not good with humor, then stay away from it and use sincerity and knowledge of the topic instead as a way to reach your audience. We bring up an additional caution about humor. Unlike the old days, today's savvy audiences are much more particular about what is humorous and what is not. Many people are, indeed, sensitive to off-color jokes, racist or sexist humor, or humor that exceeds the bounds of decorum. Don't push your luck about what you think an audience might find funny. When in doubt, don't say it.

On the other hand, a speaker who is naturally funny can use humor as an effective tool to create interaction, and there are some speech trainers who view humor as the ultimate rapport builder. Regina Barreca's book, *I Used to Be Called Snow White . . . But I Drifted* (1991), is a very funny book about women's use of humor. We suggest that you read this book if you would like to understand gender differences in the use of humor, or if you would like some instruction on the ways that gendered humor affects people. Barreca's anthology, *The Penguin Book of Women's Humor* (1996), is a good source for humorous quotations. We will say that audiences who are laughing are often audiences who are genuinely enjoying themselves and may be learning a lot as well. A person who uses humor effectively in her public speaking is Tipper Gore ("Voters Describe," 2000).

An obvious way to create interaction with an audience is to talk directly to the people. If you walk onto a stage, put both arms in the air, and say, "Hello, New York (or whatever city you are in), how are you?" the audience is sure to answer you. This kind of overt involvement pumps up the energy level. Asking rhetorical questions, requesting that the audience repeat a phrase with you, asking for a show of hands, or naming people in the audience that you know are all techniques for creating interaction. In the fall of 1996, the woman who was the epitome of interaction was Elizabeth Dole. In her campaign appearances, starting with the Republican National Convention, she adopted what communication professors and media commentators dubbed "The Oprah Style" (a more conversational, personal style). And Dole used her Oprah Winfrey style to incredible effect. She arrived at the event wearing a lapel microphone connected to a wireless system. She told the audience she liked a different style, and then came down off the stage and into the aisles. The lapel microphone allowed her the freedom to shake hands with individual audience members and walk around the room. Their attention stayed riveted on her as she delivered a memorized speech that was part storytelling, part recitation of fact and policy, and part campaign promise. She used rhetorical questions ("Wouldn't you agree?" and "It's a defining moment, isn't it?") and looked people right in the eye as a way to sustain interaction (Dole, 1996). Elizabeth Dole bears the mark of an experienced public speaker who has spent many years perfecting her skills on the public platform. Her interactive style is a brilliant strategy that she also seems to enjoy.

We mentioned earlier that interaction can also occur internally as an audience member engages in thinking about what the speaker is saying. This kind of cognitive interaction is best set up by a message that contains logic and good supporting arguments. Study the chapter on speech preparation in your primary textbook to guide you on a technical level to prepare an appealing speech. We should also mention that

---

CELL PHONE NIGHTMARE

New technology may compete for attention. Cell phones are showing up everywhere, including women's handbags and backpacks. Professor Natalle and her colleagues recently entertained a guest speaker at the university who spent most of her evening excusing herself to make personal and business telephone calls rather than interacting with her hosts and audience. Given that the speaker received an honorarium of $2,500 plus expenses, we were not amused by this behavior, and the speaker failed to build rapport with the audience. Turn off your telephone or beeper before entering a public speaking situation as a courtesy to others. If you are the speaker, ask the meeting coordinator to remind audience members to turn off cell phones. Should a phone ring during your presentation, a simple pause will turn the spotlight on the audience member's phone conversation, a surefire way to make certain the call ends quickly.

internal interaction can arise from emotional response. Bringing an audience to tears, which both Mary Fisher and Nancy Reagan accomplished at the 1996 Republican National Convention, is certainly a form of audience interaction. Finally, working an audience may include a question-and-answer session (Q & A) after the speech has been delivered. The skills involved in handling Q & A are numerous and require some practice. A complete discussion of Q & A can be found at the end of Chapter Three where we treat it as a delivery technique.

Working With an Audience Over Time

There may be an occasion when you are invited to work with an organization or group over a period of time. A likely situation would be an invitation to serve as a keynote and honored guest at a convention where you are interacting with small and large groups of people during the course of several days. This is a speaking assignment that requires versatility and patience, because everyone wants something from you, and the spotlight is likely to be directed toward you every time you step out of your hotel room. Remember, however, that you are being paid (or remunerated in some other way) because of your knowledge or position, so be ready to work hard.

One typical sequence of appearances is to give a formal keynote address sometime on the first day of the conference; appear with one or two small groups during the next day or two; and finally appear at a banquet as an honored guest on the last evening of the conference. Between appearances, convention guests will expect to see you at social activities and to be available to listen to their comments, problems, or requests for information or help. It is sometimes amazing to hear what people ask of a convention keynote—everything from professional advice concerning a son or daughter to requests for a job. Diplomacy and tact are only two of the versatility skills needed. Most importantly, cultivate your active listening skills. Even though you are speaking as a hired personality, people want to talk to you. Often, convention guests make a decision to attend because of the keynote speaker. It is an opportunity for some "up close and personal" interaction with a VIP, and you need to fill the role of that very important person with all the expertise, grace, and personality that goes with being in the spotlight.

And never go anywhere without business cards. Not only will convention guests press their own cards into your hand, but people will request your card with the intention of following up after the convention. Many people do follow up during the next couple of weeks, so do not miss an opportunity for further work. A second suggestion is to carry a small notebook at all times. Convention guests will often give you unsolicited examples and experiences relating to your area of expertise or the topic of the keynote address. You may want to jot down these conversations to add to your information files at home.

Conference speakers often enjoy a weekend vacation as part of the invitation. You will receive an honorarium. In addition, transportation, hotel, and food are often paid for by the organization. Frequently, a spouse or guest of yours may be invited, but just as often, no such courtesy is extended. If you decide to attend with a companion, then your guest should fully expect to occupy himself or herself with other activities and to pay any differences in travel and lodging costs. The quickest way to cut off future opportunities is to bring an indiscreet guest or to neglect your own duties as an honored guest of the organization. Do not forget that you are expected to mill around and be available informally, so you must make decisions about how much time to be available between scheduled appearances.

Professor Natalle once attended a small academic conference where she observed a keynote speaker make several mistakes. The keynoter was expected to appear on a panel during the first day and then give the keynote speech at the luncheon banquet the next day. Many of the conference guests expected to talk to the speaker informally at the cocktail party on the first evening and in between sessions or panels throughout the day-and-a-half conference. Unfortunately, the speaker made every mistake possible. First, she decided not to fly (causing problems with travel expenses and a forfeited plane fare) in favor of driving to the conference with her spouse, who had serious family business to attend to in the same city as the conference. Second, she decided to spend her time with her spouse and his family situation, so she was only present for the required panel appearance and the luncheon. At the panel, her interaction with the audience appeared unprepared and less than thought provoking. Even her personal appearance was criticized, as she looked to have rushed into the hotel room, showered, and run down to the room where the panel was scheduled. Finally, the speaker did not appear at the cocktail party or in any other informal capacity. Conference guests kept asking where she was, and many were disappointed not to have the opportunity to interact with a scholar who was largely admired and respected in the field. The happy ending to this story is that the keynote address was very good, and she lived up to her reputation both as a scholar and as a public speaker. Her speech was well prepared and addressed the conference theme with adaptation. Although the speaker fulfilled her main duty, we are recommending that you meet the expectations of an audience in a manner that goes above and beyond the example just noted.

Our final words of advice: Do your homework. Audience analysis can make or break the success of your speech.

Chapter Three

Delivering the Message

In Tennessee, the publishers of a business directory *(Doing Business in Memphis)* offer custom-designed workshops on a variety of business topics. On their website (http://www.memphisbusiness.com/dbim/services.html), they describe their seminars as follows: "Our teaching and consulting approach to these topics is practical, 'hands on,' and example-driven. We are not 'in your face' motivational gurus. You will find no one jumping up on chairs and no silly games. Sorry, no group hugs, either. Our style is low-key, humorous when appropriate, with our full concentration upon your employees and how they relate to the topic being presented." We couldn't agree more. Like the consulting approach described above, good speech delivery does not involve gimmicks or flash. Interesting and engaging presentations come from careful preparation of both content and delivery.

For us, delivering the message involves three phases: before, during, and after. In this chapter, we'll cover these three phases, paying particular attention to nonverbal and verbal communication strategies that help build credibility. First, we'll discuss rehearsing, handling stage fright, and what to wear on the day of the presentation. Next, we'll cover voice, nonverbal communication, and handling the podium. We'll also address what happens once the speech is over, and you are asked to take questions (Q & A) from the audience. But first, let's discuss some preliminary issues you should be aware of regarding gender and the delivery of a speech.

Gender and Credibility

Nancy Austin is a management consultant and author. In 1985, she cowrote *A Passion for Excellence: The Leadership Difference* with Tom Peters, an internationally known management expert and bestselling author. Austin's clients include AT&T, Toyota, Hewlett Packard, and a host of other well-known corporations. In short, Austin is a successful and intelligent woman. Yet, after delivering a speech, the feedback she receives is more often about her physical appearance than her ideas. She reflects on that situation in the following passage:

> The margins for what's acceptable for women (presenters) are more narrow. I've gotten anonymous feedback generally on some feature of my appearance . . . This is the most consistent form of feedback I get, by the way—comments on hair, clothing, shoes, jewelry. That's very common, very, very common . . . and it comes from women. I wonder, "Did you hear the speech? What did you think about that?" . . . Tom [Peters] gets feedback, but it's a different kind of thing. He'll generate heated discussion but there's a basic respect. With women it isn't that way, there's a little more room there to be negative. (Austin, 1996, p. 18)

Why would an accomplished woman like Nancy Austin not earn the same respect as her male coauthor, Tom Peters? When we don't know someone particularly well, just as an audience does not know a speaker personally, we may make judgments about that person based on the information that is immediately obvious or visible—race, age, and gender, for example. Making quick judgments is a natural reaction when we meet a new person. Suppose, for example, you are about to meet a coworker who was just hired. Your friend at work describes the new person as: tall with short dark hair, chiseled features, and a passion for auto racing and ice fishing. Who did you picture? Did you assume the coworker was a man? Even from this brief description, you probably made assumptions about this person—the same thing happens whenever we meet someone for the first time.

Psychology professor Linda Carli writes, "In American culture, race, class, education, age, occupation, physical attractiveness, and gender can act as *diffuse status characteristics*, characteristics of a person that are used, particularly in the absence of specific information, to assess his or her competence, ability or value. People with relatively high status are expected to be more competent, to perform better, and to have more desirable attributes than low status individuals; they are also given more opportunities to perform well and are consequently more influential" (1990, p. 941).

A HISTORY NOTE

Kathleen Hall Jamieson writes that as recently as the nineteenth century, a woman who was "hysterical," that is a woman who "paid too little attention to detail, expressed too much emotion, and was flamboyant," was given "The Rest Cure." Women under the care of Dr. S. Weir, who pioneered the cure, received instructions to rest and "control their urges to express their feelings to others" (p. 72). While bed rest may sound tempting to today's busy women, we can more freely express our emotions, ideas, attitudes, and beliefs than at any time in history—a reward for which we can thank all the women public speakers who charted new territory before our time.

(Source: Kathleen Hall Jamieson. (1988). *Eloquence in an Electronic Age: The Transformation of Political Speechmaking*. New York: Oxford University Press, pp. 71–73.)

Women have made great strides in the last several years toward equality, increasing their status in the workplace and in other arenas that were previously closed to them. And we certainly are miles ahead of the women who are described by Kathleen Hall Jamieson in the box above. Still, as communication and gender scholar Julia Wood tells us: "To be masculine is to be strong, ambitious, successful, rational, and emotionally controlled . . . To be feminine is to be physically attractive, deferential, unaggressive, emotional, nurturing, and concerned with people and relationships" (2003, p. 22). What Professor Wood is saying is that even though we as individuals may be entertaining different ideas about how to shape and enact our gender roles, society's perception of masculinity and femininity is still grounded in old-fashioned stereotypes. When we look at the variables associated with high status (such as competence and high levels of performance) and the characteristics associated with masculinity (such as strength and success), we can see a strong correlation—men are still given higher status in our society than women (Bradley, 1981; Carli, 1990). As a public speaker and a woman, you must be aware of these issues if you are to make good choices for yourself.

So, what does this mean for a woman public speaker? It does not mean that every time a woman voices her ideas, no one is listening, or that women are not getting a fair hearing. But, persons with high status, including men, are seen as more effective in persuasion. Communication scholar Judy Pearson and her colleagues (Pearson, Turner, & Todd-Mancillas, 1991) report that when identical messages are delivered by men and women, men are typically judged as more persuasive. Therefore, women who speak in public must employ a variety of strategies to build their credibility. Men must take time to build their credibility with the audience too; for example, both women and men are more likely to influence their audience when they use supporting materials (see your textbook). But a woman may need to pay special attention to her choice of language, appearance, gestures, and other aspects of content and delivery in order to have maximum influence on the audience. With that in mind, let's now turn to the three phases of delivery.

Before the Speech

Once, while teaching a public speaking class, Professor Bodenheimer realized that her students were performing below the level expected for that point in the semester. In an attempt to discover what was causing this poor performance, I asked the students to write a paragraph on their rehearsal habits—how often they rehearsed, how far in advance they rehearsed, if they timed themselves, and so on. One young woman, who seemed particularly disorganized every time she gave a speech in class, wrote, "I never practice actually *saying* (emphasis added) my speech, but I do read it over and over! I try to memorize as I write, but most of the time I just get confused!" No wonder she got confused. She had never actually said her speech aloud until the moment she reached the podium.

There are several basic steps to run through before you get up to give a speech, and the chapter on delivery in your primary textbook is designed to assist you with this. For both women and men, we cannot emphasize enough the need to practice out loud in front of a mirror and in front of friends and family. We know that five or six run-throughs are better than one. Having appropriate note cards is a must. Timing your speech is essential, especially if you are given a limited amount of time for the delivery of the speech—and this is usually the case. Practicing with your intended visual aids will smooth delivery. And, of course, the ultimate luxury is having access to the physical location where you will speak so that you can check out the facility and do a dry run. But, there are specific aspects of preplanning that have implications for the gender of the speaker. Apprehension and clothes are two areas that need discussion.

Conquering Stage Fright

For as long as people have been speaking in public, they have been devising methods for reducing stage fright. You may have heard the one about picturing the audience members in their underwear. If this method or any other strategy works for you, use it. But, in general, there are no special tricks for eliminating the jitters. Being entirely familiar with your topic and rehearsing your speech are the most essential tools for dealing with speech anxiety. A little stage fright, however, is healthy and perfectly normal for women and men. Even experienced speakers get a little nervous before a speaking engagement. Communication apprehension is fear or anxiety about communicating with others, and most Americans regularly list public speaking as one of the top five things they are afraid of, right up there with going to the dentist and dying ("Scaredy Cats," 1997).

Communication researchers (McCroskey, Simpson, & Richmond, 1982) have tested the idea that women may be more apprehensive than men about getting up in front of an audience to give a speech. Studies show that women tend to score higher on apprehension tests, but the actual differences in level of apprehension between men and women is statistically quite small. Nevertheless, women think they are afraid and seem to have a different mind-set about fear of public speaking.

FIRST TIME JITTERS

Even the most confident speakers have experienced stage fright. Patricia Ireland, former president of the National Organization for Women, described her first terrifying experience before an audience. At the time, Ireland was in law school and trying to gather signatures for a petition aimed at the publisher of the textbook that was being used in her property law class. She wanted to protest the line that read, "Land, like a woman, is meant to be possessed."

Rounding up a large number of signatures person by person would take too long. I'd have to address a large group and ask people to sign all at once. So, hands shaking and voice trembling, I called the hundred or so members of my property law class to order one day before our professor arrived and read them my statement. Seeing all those tired pairs of eyes centered on me—expecting me to come up with a very good reason to interrupt their pre-class gossip or study—nearly ended my public speaking career on the spot.

From *What Women Want*, 1996, pp. 70–71

Thank goodness the first-time jitters didn't get the best of her.

In a study by Stowell and Furlong (1995), students at a community college were asked to write about their feelings on public speaking by completing the following sentence: "Giving a speech makes me feel..." Although the results suggested that men were slightly more at ease in front of the microphone, the more intriguing findings concern the reasons students had for feeling nervous. The researchers discovered that "more than half of the women wrote about being judged by the audience" (p. 5). More specifically, women wrote about being looked at, using phrases such as "all eyes are on me" and "being stared at" (p. 5). In contrast, only one man wrote about being stared at, and five men actually used the term *adrenaline rush* to describe their public speaking experiences.

Stowell and Furlong concluded that female students judge their own speech-giving skills based on how others perceive them, in part because of the strong media and cultural influences that suggest a woman must be attractive to be liked. This seems realistic when you recall Nancy Austin's experience described earlier. Stowell and Furlong stated "that female students judge their ability (competency) to stand and deliver a speech based on how the audience appears to be receiving them: focusing on issues related to how do I look, what are they thinking of me, do I look nervous, do I appear to be knowledgeable and prepared, etc." (p. 7). In contrast, men look inward and base their competency judgments on "how do I look to myself."

In the process of worrying over what others think of them, young girls self-monitor to the point of muting themselves. In his essay, "Young Voices Lost" (1994), Robert Johnson writes of his experience teaching at a private girls school. Young women who were bright, competent, creative, and communicative in class completely changed when male peers entered the room. They became submissive and acted giggly. The same girls who could kid with Johnson and call him a "fat old fart" actually "shriveled" when young males their own age were present.

Johnson asked his students to write essays about this change in communication behavior. One student wrote that girls should not sound "intellectually threatening" around males, and another suggested that girls should downplay their academic successes. Another young woman wrote about participating in a complicated physics discussion after class. Referring to one of the young men in the discussion, she wrote that it "blew his mind" that a woman could keep up. Regarding her goals as a speaker, one of Johnson's students wrote, "My general aim is to leave everyone with the opinion of me as a polite, intelligent young person, and if I am to know them longer than an hour or so, it is nice for them to think I am funny or interesting." Although this sounds appropriate for any public speaker, most of these girls were far more interested in practicing their own ideas of femininity, which included the notions of "being passive, soft-spoken, polite . . . no longer assertive." Further, the girls wanted to be "agreeable and not contradict anything a man says." Johnson's students were not far off the mark because there are studies (Carli, LaFleur, & Loeber, 1995) that indicate women have to be liked if they want their message to be heard.

Physical appearance and fitting in are closely tied to self-esteem, and there is no question that both men and women who have high levels of self-esteem are going to be more comfortable sharing their ideas. The connection between self-esteem and a willingness to communicate is well established (Richmond & McCroskey, 1985). In the early nineties, the American Association of University Women (AAUW) published a comprehensive report entitled *Shortchanging Girls, Shortchanging America.* The Caucasian girls in the study somehow lost their self-esteem between grade school and high school. At ages eight and nine, 60 percent of the girls reported being "happy the way I am," but by high school only 29 percent said they were happy with themselves. Forty-six percent of high school boys were happy with the way they were, and they had more willingness than girls to "speak out, speak up in class, and argue with the teacher" when they thought they were right. An interesting note is that African American girls did not experience significant drops in their levels of self-esteem throughout grade school and high school. The AAUW criticized the teachers for some of the disparity in self-esteem levels that was observed between the Caucasian boys and girls. The teachers tended to talk to boys more, encourage boys more, and listen more when boys called out in class. In contrast, when girls called out, teachers told them to raise their hands if they wished to speak (AAUW, 1991, 1992).

In the best-selling book *Reviving Ophelia* (1994), another study about adolescent girls and self-esteem, author Mary Pipher described young girls in a more disturbing way: "Their voices have gone underground—their speech is more tentative and less articulate" (p. 20). Pipher suggests that many adult women continue to struggle with these same issues. Some of you may be a part of the generation of women described by the AAUW or Mary Pipher. If you have a strong fear of presenting yourself on the public platform, it is possible there are links to your experiences as a high school girl. Wondering if we look good, if we are liked, and if we sound competent is naturally going to make us nervous because these are things we can't control. So, what can you do to gain control of your fear and your voice? The key is to keep stage fright at a level that you can manage successfully.

Even though your primary textbook has advice for dealing with communication apprehension, we want to reinforce some techniques that will help women think outside the box of fear that we often put ourselves in. Speaking of fear, examine the box below and see what you think about the way the federal government reinforces fear with stereotyped advertising.

WOMEN'S COMMUNICATION TRAINING IN THE FEDERAL GOVERNMENT

U.S. News & World Report carried a news brief about the U.S. Department of Agriculture's class called Communications Skills for Women. This course costs $129 and is advertised with the following blurb: "Don't let your fear of communicating with authority impact and prevent you from accomplishing your professional and personal goals. Recognize and overcome the sex-role stereotypes that may be holding you back. Position yourself for growth and advancement. Work to avoid speech mannerisms and appearance mistakes that mark you as 'lightweight.'"

(Source: Paul Bedard, Suzi Parker, David E. Kaplan, & Richard J. Newman. (2000, December 18). Fear of Flying? *U.S. News & World Report, 129,* 10.)

The first and most important technique for dealing with the pre-speech jitters is to know your topic, know your topic, know your topic. You should know more about your topic than you ever plan to say in your speech. If you are confident that you know your topic thoroughly, inside and out, you will feel confident in front of the microphone. Think about it. If we asked you to get up right now and give a five-minute presentation on the intricacies of your job or your favorite hobby or pastime, you would walk right to the podium and start talking, before you even had time to get nervous. Knowing your topic is like packing a suitcase with all of those "just in case" items: an umbrella, extra contact lenses, a bottle of aspirin. You hope you don't need them, but you feel better just knowing they are tucked away in your carry-on luggage. It is the same with your speech. It may not be necessary to know every fact about your topic, but the more you have tucked away in your mind, the better you'll feel. Besides, you often need to draw on that knowledge during the question-and-answer period, so it doesn't hurt to have facts stored away.

Channel the adrenaline rushing through your system into your speech, rather than using it to get worked up or worried. Focus on connecting your topic to the audience, instead of focusing on yourself.

After all, you have something important to say to that particular audience, or you wouldn't be on the agenda.

And remember, most audiences are friendly, even if they don't agree with your point of view. In the thousands of speeches we have heard, we have never seen one tomato thrown. Even if you do experience a hostile audience (see Chapter Two for techniques for dealing with a hostile audience) or the occasional heckler, you will remain in control if you know your topic well enough.

Some people like to use a technique to reduce stage fright called visualization. The basic premise behind this method is to picture yourself as a success. As you prepare in the weeks before the presentation, imagine yourself getting up the day of the speech, putting on a great outfit, arriving effortlessly at the facility where you will deliver your speech, walking with ease to the podium, and talking through the beginning, middle, and end of your speech to the sound of thundering applause.

Of course, visualization must be balanced with realistic expectations. Setting realistic expectations may help you fight stage fright before it even begins. You want to deliver a great speech, getting all of your points across in a compelling way. But delivering a great speech does not mean perfection, especially for beginning speakers. It is realistic to think you may stumble over a word, forget a small point you wanted to make, or lose your place. As human beings communicating with other human beings, it is only natural to have a few minor flaws in an otherwise great presentation.

Take A Deep Breath

While all of the techniques for managing stage fright in the previous section focus on preparing yourself mentally for the speech, your body also plays an important role. For example, some women find that taking a series of deep breaths or doing stretching exercises before the presentation helps to calm them. Singing or humming in the shower can help warm up your voice and get out some of your nervous energy. Even more fundamentally, a good night's sleep the evening before your presentation will do wonders for calming your nerves.

If you find that you get a dry mouth or throat before a speech, take a sip of water or another clear liquid like apple juice. Avoid milk, soda, orange juice, or other thicker liquids that may coat your vocal mechanism and not allow it to work properly. This is especially important to keep in mind if you are invited to share a meal with the audience members before the speech. Also, there's nothing wrong with taking your glass of water with you to the podium, in case of a tickle or cough during delivery of the speech. Professor Bodenheimer attended a workshop where the famous linguist Deborah Tannen was the featured speaker (2001). During her presentation, Dr. Tannen's voice cracked and she had a coughing fit. Her experience as a speaker paid off. Tannen reached for her water and humorously told the audience to "talk among yourselves" while she regained composure.

Above all, even if you feel a bit nervous, don't let it show, and certainly don't call attention to it. "Good Morning. I am a little nervous today, so I hope you will bear with me" is not exactly attention getting and may give the audience the impression that you are not really worth a listen.

I Haven't Got a Thing to Wear

Whether it is politically correct or not, and whether we like it not, a speaker's appearance makes an impact on the audience's perception of that speaker and the speaker's message. Do you remember the criticism prosecuting attorney Marcia Clark endured when she changed her hairstyle during the course of the O. J. Simpson trial? There is a real connection between appearance and credibility, and we have known this since the mid-1960s when Mills and Aronson (1965) found that female speakers in attractive dress were more successful at persuading audiences than women who had a "repulsive" appearance. Consider, for example, a businesswoman, with whom Professor Bodenheimer worked, who was preparing to deliver a day-long workshop. The businesswoman had more than fifteen years experience with the topic that she was addressing. She also was blonde, tall, pretty, looked quite young, and had legs about which most women can only dream. Unfortunately, her voice had a slight nasal quality. Get the picture? Her voice and appearance added up to the quintessential stereotype of the dumb blonde; although, in reality, the speaker was bright and quite competent. Adding to this speaker's challenge was the fact that most of the registered workshop participants were men.

Although this particular presenter had to use many strategies to boost her credibility, the one we want to focus on here is the careful planning of her presentation day wardrobe. Audience members in any situation will, consciously or not, begin to form a favorable or unfavorable impression of the speaker based simply on appearance, before a single word is even spoken. In this case, the speaker had to remain true to her style and yet deliver the message that she was confident, able, and knowledgeable. Showing up in a mid-calf length dress with a floral print, high collar, and lace trim may have made the speaker look more dowdy and less sexy, but she would have hardly felt confident wearing clothes so different from her usual outfits (tastefully short and form-fitting clothes). Instead, on presentation day, she chose a neutral-colored business suit and wore eyeglasses and minimal jewelry.

How you dress on the day of your speech will be determined, in part, by the public speaking situation. You wouldn't want to show up in the corporate boardroom wearing jeans and a cropped T-shirt to give a financial report. Similarly, you wouldn't want to deliver a report on dwindling profits to workers on the factory floor wearing a red Chanel suit. In both cases, you want to look polished to deliver an important message, but in two very different ways. A good general rule is to wear something that is just a bit dressier than what the majority of the audience members are wearing. For example, at many conferences, the style of dress is business casual (a style which in itself has many interpretations). As a featured speaker, you would want to wear a simple business suit or dress with matching jacket, or a skirt and a blazer. College students, in particular, are faced with the challenge of "appropriate" clothes. The fashions right now include clothes that are sometimes very revealing—low-cut tanks, thin straps, bare midriffs, tight-fitting fabrics, and short skirts. None of this is right for public speaking. Resist the notion of looking sexy, and cover the body so that the audience can concentrate on your speech content.

Several years ago companies started the practice of casual Friday. The *Los Angeles Times* ("Managing in the Next," 1996) estimated that over 90 percent of workplaces have some form of a casual Friday or a casual dress code. A survey cited in the article said that over half the female respondents felt they lost status and authority when dressed casually. One woman wrote: "Men can afford to be more casual without losing their power and authority. Women still need more props" (p. 11). An African American female manager at Nissan Motor Company added, "When you look the part, some people will think you're doing the part" (p. 11). *Dress for Success* author John Molloy confirms the *Los Angeles Times* survey by arguing that women, minorities, and short men may all have their authority undercut by casual wear because they are not the people that mainstream society sees as leaders or managers (McPherson, 1997). Tall white males seem to have the advantage in the casual wear practices of the workplace, and these same rules apply to the speaking platform.

Remember that dressing up does not mean that a simple business suit has to translate into a boring or plain outfit. And, you certainly are not limited to a navy blue suit. There isn't a right or wrong color to wear—you know what looks best on you. If you don't, have a color analysis done. Many cosmetics companies offer this service, and it is well worth the price of the cosmetics that you will probably buy anyway. We do, however, recommend that you stay away from pastels, especially under studio lighting. Pale pink or blue, and mint green, tend to wash out. Go with darker shades and do not be afraid to wear deep purple, red, or royal blue. Rich colors often set off jewelry. Although we are not endorsing any product line, there are many brand-name clothes that are affordable, stylish, and do not wrinkle. Several chain department stores across the country offer seasonal suits that will serve you for many years. (Professor Natalle is not afraid to admit she is a clothes collector. I have items in my closet that I have collected over a twenty-five-year period. They are well cared for and are a part of my platform persona.) If you can afford to spend money on a good suit, do so. While you are shopping, do not ignore shoes. Our best recommendation is for color coordination and good fit. Tired feet have a way of dragging you down. Aching feet soon become aching legs, and your overall energy level tends to drop. Stay away from high heels as much as possible—they are neither comfortable nor healthy. We give this advice on shoes knowing that many women insist on high heels, but if you spend as much time on the public platform as we do, you will agree that a low heel is better.

Do add scarves, jewelry, or other minimal accessories as long as they are not distracting. Take time to find a good hair stylist and get a cut that complements your face and bone structure. Hair is just as much a fashion accessory as makeup and jewelry. Scarves with busy patterns, large jewelry, or other dangling accessories fall into the distraction category. For example, Professor Bodenheimer once wore a charm bracelet to deliver a presentation. According to a friend in the audience, every time I gestured the charms jingled, distracting the audience from what I was saying. Dangle earrings and multiple bracelets are not good choices. Quiet jewelry works better. If you are making the transition from college to the work world, then it is time to develop a professional style that matches the career field to which you aspire. Finally, if you are not confident about your fashion sense, ask for a consultation with a personal shopper at a better department store. Overall, clothes are a wise investment for a public speaker; appearance will have an impact on how the audience perceives the message.

You may now be wondering if we are attempting to turn all of you into middle-class clones. Fear not! Remember our concern for persona? Dress and self-presentation are part of that public persona. If, for example, ethnic clothing is a part of your personal image or an audience expectation, we are not suggesting that you abandon your trademarks. Rather, we are suggesting some general principles based on our experiences and observations. Remember Nancy Austin's experience

(DILBERT reprinted by permission of United Feature Syndicate, Inc.)

cited in the beginning of this chapter? If one of the goals is to increase credibility, then take our advice about the general level of conservatism in American audiences. If you plan to serve in a public office or work for the government, the National Women's Political Caucus also suggests a conservative approach to appearance in their 1995 campaign guidebook.

In an opinion piece for the *Washington Post*, Richard Cohen (1997) wrote a matter-of-fact analysis about the lack of support for Ruth Messinger in her race against Rudolph Giuliani for mayor of New York City. Point blank, Democrats were penalizing Messinger because she was not glamorous enough as a mayoral candidate. This is pure sexism and hard-core reality. It seems that credibility is best increased by conforming, as much as is appropriate to your comfort level, to the general public's expectations for the American woman in a two-piece suit. Our hope is that you spend a reasonable amount of time developing an appropriate look, just as we suggest that you spend a reasonable amount of time on speech preparation.

BEAUTY OR BRAINS?

Rose Elizabeth Bird ran two campaigns during the 1980s for chief justice of the California Supreme Court. She was described as "dowdy" in the first campaign, but after undergoing a dramatic transformation in personal appearance, she was labeled "stunningly beautiful" in the second campaign. A group of researchers concluded that Bird's attractiveness indirectly made an impact on her electability because voters equated attractiveness with femininity, effectiveness, and interpersonal appeal, thus improving her chances of being elected.

(Source: Lee Sigelman, Carol Sigelman, & Christopher Fowler. (1987). A Bird of a Different Feather? An Experimental Investigation of Physical Attractiveness and the Electability of Female Candidates. *Social Psychology Quarterly*, 50, 32–43.)

During the Speech

Stand Up Straight

Believe it or not, the "during part" of your speech actually begins before you ever make your way to the front of the room, especially if you are the keynote speaker or a featured guest. Once you have been identified as a speaker, panelist, or a facilitator, the audience members will be watching you. In effect, you are "on," even while sitting down waiting for the program to begin or in the ladies' room.

Once you do make your way to the podium (or down from the podium as Elizabeth Dole did during the 1996 Republican National Convention), remember what your mother told you: Stand up straight! Not only does good posture help your vocal mechanism work properly, it may help to make a favorable impression on the audience. In a study by psychology professor Don Osborn, participants were asked to view pictures of two women, one normal weight and the other underweight, standing sideways, each in three different poses: rigid, normal, and slumped. Participants identified the women standing up straight, regardless of weight, as more attractive. Osborn concluded, "I hear so many young girls talk about how much better they'd look if they lost ten or fifteen pounds. This study shows they'd be more attractive if they just stood up straight" (Newman, 1997, p. 82). And, as we already know, a speaker's appearance does affect the audience's perception of her. So, walk to the front of the room with confidence and poise. A slight hesitation, a slow walk, a dour expression, or slumped shoulders may give the audience doubts before you ever open your mouth. Don't worry if your hands are trembling or your stomach is turning somersaults. The audience can't see this. What they do see is a confident woman with something to say.

SMILING: A WOMAN'S MOST CONTROVERSIAL EXPRESSION

In a discussion on gender and nonverbal expression, communication scholar Julia Wood reports that Caucasian women, in particular, use excessive smiling as a show of response, friendliness, and interest in others. If she is not smiling, others may perceive something to be wrong. Can a woman be happy without smiling? Of course! The problem lies in how much smiling is necessary, both as an expression of emotion and as a cue to others. Society teaches women to smile as part of their public presentation of self, so you may wish to think about your own smiling habits and what they mean to audiences.

(Source: Julia T. Wood. (2003). *Gendered Lives*. 5th ed. Belmont, CA: Wadsworth, p. 133.)

As you begin to speak, take a deep breath and smile. And we do mean a deep breath. Breathe from the diaphragm, not the lungs. You must have plenty of breath to carry your words, so short bursts from the chest just won't be enough. Put your fingertips on your diaphragm area (located in the center torso below the rib cage) and practice breathing deeply. Getting used to this deep breathing technique will pay off when trying to use your voice and vocal qualities to your best advantage. Why do we suggest smiling? There is some evidence that pleasant facial expressions, including smiles, send endorphins to the brain and put you in a positive mood. If this is true, then it can't hurt to enjoy yourself.

Now that you have made your way to the front of the room, your voice and body will become important tools. While dynamic delivery is no substitute for interesting and well researched content, effective delivery can enhance a speaker's message. In the next sections, we'll discuss using your voice and body to add power and credibility to your speech.

Speak Up

Just as the words in a speech are of primary importance, so is the vocal delivery of those words. Your voice is a tool that needs training for best effect, and your primary textbook contains useful information to help you get started. For example, you will learn some standard rules about appropriate rate of speech, articulation of sound, correct pronunciation, use of dialect, volume, and pitch. Several aspects of voice have gender implications.

The pitch of your voice refers to its highness or lowness, as on a musical scale. Nonverbal communication researcher Dale Leathers (1992) reported that women's vocal cords are generally shorter than men's, thus accounting for women's higher modal pitch. This is a true biological difference between the sexes. When speaking in public, nervousness can result in a slightly higher pitch, compounding the problem for women. For example, former Congresswoman Susan Molinari's keynote speech at the 1996 Republican National Convention was upbeat and fast-paced, but her pitch was slightly higher than normal. There is a theoretical perspective (Henley, 1977) that says women use higher pitch as a socially learned way of projecting femininity in their speaking. If this is true, then Molinari's error at the podium may have been a result of nerves, biology, and learned behavior.

Some women also use a pattern where their pitch rises by the end of a sentence so that a statement may sound like a question. This could lead to misinterpretation of meaning, or a judgment by the audience that the speaker is unsure of herself. Neither result is desired by a speaker. Try listening to a favorite newscaster, such as Jane Pauley of NBC or Carol Simpson of ABC, as a good role model for appropriate pitch and all-around vocal inflection.

Our society retains some old stereotypes that prefer a male voice over a female voice. On television in the mid-1980s, men performed between 80 and 90 percent of voice-overs for advertisements (Cropper, 1998). In the 1990s, the Screen Actors Guild launched a campaign entitled "Women as Voices of Persuasion and Authority" to encourage more advertisers to use women's voices ("Screen Actors," 1996). Clifford Nass, a Stanford University communication professor, has conducted numerous studies on voice technology. Nass (Eisenberg, 2000) found that when two speakers read the same set of directions, the male voice is perceived to be more accurate. A male voice is also perceived as slightly more informative when talking about technical information. Nass predicts that voice technology, such as talking web pages in automobiles that give directions, will be dominated by deep male voices. The research cited here leaves no doubt that gender and voice are interrelated in the mind of the audience and may very well affect judgments of speaker credibility.

In addition to using your voice for the best effect, there are numerous nonverbal strategies a speaker can employ to enhance her message and credibility. While we often don't think about gestures or facial expressions, these actions send important messages in themselves. In other words, voice, eye contact, and body movements are all factors that may influence the audience's overall perception of what you have to say. In fact, we like to think about verbal and nonverbal communication as two components that make up the whole package, or message. As a speaker, you must attend to developing both types of tools. In the next two sections, we'll discuss eye contact, gestures and movement, and the use of a podium.

Create Connection

In general, says psychologist Linda Carli and her colleagues (1995), the speaker who has upright posture, maintains a high level of eye contact (without staring), eliminates verbal stumbles or hesitations, and uses purposeful but restrained gestures is perceived by the audience as competent. In contrast, speakers who slump, speak too slowly, sustain little eye contact, use a soft voice, and frequently hesitate or stumble over words will be perceived by the audience as less competent.

For women speakers, however, competence may not be enough, especially with a male audience. Carli's research team has indicated that women speakers also need to be liked in order to influence the audience. How can you demonstrate to the audience that you are likable? Chances are you are already doing it. Women in our society are socialized to "respond expressively to others" (Carli, LaFleur, & Loeber, 1995). Caucasian women in particular are expected to maintain eye contact and smile (communication acts which express emotion); when we don't, others may think something is wrong or out of the ordinary. Eye contact, smiling, and other expressive behaviors (such as positive head nodding) communicate friendliness and show rapport. Therefore, a combination of these nonverbal behaviors with those that demonstrate competence may be just the right mix for maximum influence on the audience.

Elizabeth Dole is a good example of a speaker who uses these friendly behaviors to her advantage. Yes, they are what the audience expects from a woman, but Dole does not use them because she feels obligated to behave in a particular way to please the audience. Rather she uses them quite purposefully to get the audience exactly where she wants them, every time. This technique is called creating immediacy, and it is part of the general concern a speaker has for creating rapport with an audience. (See Chapter Six for more about Dole's use of immediacy in creating her public persona.)

Movement is another aspect of creating immediacy. You will want to avoid endless pacing, but you may want to move closer to the audience to, for example, emphasize a point or to tell a personal story. Moving away from your notes for your entire presentation takes practice, and this style of speaking is better left for more experienced speakers. But if you do plan to move away from your notes to deliver a section of your speech, make sure you are entirely familiar not only with that section of your speech, but with the transition into the next part, so you can safely make your way back to the podium. And similarly, don't make the mistake of dozens of speakers we have watched who move away from the podium or head table and closer to the audience, taking their index cards, papers, or a pen with them. They continue to speak and, at the same time, wave the index cards back and forth. Leave those distracting items back at the podium, especially if you are one of those people who talks with her hands. (Professor Bodenheimer—guilty as charged!) This concept also applies to clothing. If you have a necklace with which you fidget, hair you twirl, or a scarf you tug on, avoid temptation by wearing your hair another way or choosing an outfit free of fidget-prone accessories.

The Podium as a Gender Problem

The podium itself can become a serious problem for women trying to deliver a speech. Typically, male speakers grip the corners and lean on or over the podium. Keep in mind this simple tip: the podium was built for your notes, not for you. Use it to support your notes or your hands, but not your whole body. Okay, easy enough, except for one small problem: some women are too short to even see over the top of the podium. Here is a true story: Professor Natalle attended a United Way luncheon at which a featured speaker was a woman from a local adoption agency. The speaker's job was to give an informative speech telling us how contributions were used to support the agency. As she got up to speak, she asked, "Can you hear me?" The audience called out, "Yes!" She continued: "Good! Now I don't have to stand behind that podium (gesturing to it). Although you would be able to hear me through the microphone, you wouldn't be able to see me (pause), and we don't even want to go into that!" The audience laughed, and she proceeded to give a fast-paced, energetic speech that effectively informed us about the agency. Sitting in the audience, I didn't think it was so funny from the perspective of a public speaking teacher. It is a shame that women have to adapt by giving up a microphone, given that vocal problems are a common barrier in our public speaking.

Another example of a podium problem involved the famous "talking hat" incident with Queen Elizabeth. During a visit to the United States, the queen and President George H. Bush gave prepared remarks in an outdoor location where a podium and microphone were provided. President Bush was perfectly comfortable behind the podium, but when the queen stepped up to speak, all that could be seen was her hat bobbing. The queen recovered nicely with a witticism, but the moral of the incident is that public speaking equipment is often sized and arranged for speakers who are six feet tall. An interesting footnote to the podium problem: The *CBS Evening News,* on January 24, 1997, featured a news clip of a short spokeswoman preparing to come forward and speak in the White House Press Room. She used her foot to slide out a step located at the base of the podium. She then stepped up and began speaking into the microphone that was just at the right height for her. We wondered if this step was installed for people like former Labor Secretary Robert Reich, or if the Queen Elizabeth incident prompted a change. During an April 1997 interview on National Public Radio's *Fresh Air,* Robert Reich did, indeed, tell host Terry Gross that standing behind a standard podium was a problem for him because he was too short to see over the top (Reich, 1997).

Professor Natalle (who is five feet three inches tall) once solved the monster podium problem by asking a hotel employee to grab a heavy plastic glass rack out of the hotel kitchen. I turned it upside down and immediately had a six-inch riser on which to stand comfortably in flat shoes. This solution, although it limited spontaneous movement, was the only way to solve the problem at the moment. I had several hundred people sitting in a room with poor acoustics and needed to use the fixed microphone mounted on the podium. This strange, but effective, solution also reinforced the notion that flat shoes are a safety measure that make more sense than high heels as a fashion statement. Tannen (1994) reports that Maryland Senator Barbara Mikulski, who is four feet eleven inches tall, carries a footstool to public speaking engagements so that she gains authority with height behind the lectern. Although we do not recommend racks from industrial dishwashers as standard speaking equipment, we do recommend that you arrive early to check the room so that you can make adjustments if necessary. If you really do need to carry a footstool, just make sure it is safe.

Overwhelmed? It may seem like there is a lot to remember during the delivery of a speech—make eye contact, stand up straight, prepare, present, explain, pause, do gesture, don't fidget. The suggestions presented here are general guidelines intended to be used within the context of each woman's personal style. Some women are naturally more gregarious than others, smiling or gesturing frequently. For these speakers, placing their hands at their sides would be so unnatural that the flow of the entire speech would be disrupted. Without question, your personal communication style is the most successful one for you because it is you. Our best advice is for you to discover the essence of your personal style, and capitalize on the positive aspects of that style. It will mark your signature as a speaker.

After the Speech

Once you have finished speaking, you may feel exhausted or exhilarated, or if you are like most speakers, a combination of both. But, just because you have wowed the audience with a creative and insightful conclusion, doesn't necessarily mean that you are finished. Many standard public speaking texts do not give much information about how to handle post-speaking activity. Whether you are male or female, you may be required to answer questions from the audience. We suggest several techniques here to help you conduct smooth and effective Q & A. First, tell the audience whether you will take questions immediately after the speech or later in one-on-one conversations with the audience members. Second, if you take questions immediately after the speech, limit the number to just a few. People are often restless, and movement begins as some audience members leave their seats. Third, if you are in a large auditorium, try to arrange for two microphones to be placed in different, accessible locations so that questions can be heard by all, and so that people can take turns in a manageable way. Repeat the question before you answer it to ensure that everyone in the audience has heard the question. Fourth, be ready for anything in Q & A. Although most people are friendly and want further clarification of your views, there are some hostile audience members who want to pick a fight or challenge you as a way to discredit your speech. Be ready! Try to think fast but remain respectful and diplomatic, even in the face of a hostile question. If you appear irritated or crack under the pressure of an insult, you may wind up compromising the intended effects of the speech. Fifth, if you are truly not very good at answering questions in the large group setting, then you will want to make it a routine that you do not take questions after a speech. If that is the case, then provide an alternative format for answering questions if possible. Study the quick tips at the end of the chapter to improve your ability to handle Q & A.

Once questions have been answered, you may have to mingle with audience members or other speakers, or gather up workshop materials. At this point, you are probably anxious to get out of your public persona and into your private persona. But first, you'll have to leave the podium just as you approached it—with poise, a smile, and a confident walk—even if, for some reason, you feel the speech did not go as well as you had hoped. The audience may well have liked your speech and felt challenged by your ideas. Don't damage your credibility in the last few seconds by leaving the podium with a scowl on your face. Above all, don't leave the podium until you are finished talking. Too many speakers get to the last idea and begin to walk back to their seats, so by the time that creative conclusion is uttered, the speaker is practically sitting down with the audience.

Finally, when you walk off the platform, be prepared for further interaction with individual audience members. People will invariably come up to ask more questions, criticize your speech, or congratulate you. Stay energized throughout these conversations because they do leave a lasting impression on people. A tip for debriefing yourself: in your hotel room or back at home, jot down notes in the back of this handbook about what worked and what didn't. Keep this informal diary as a way to build on your strengths, find out new information, and correct problems that shouldn't get in your way as a successful public speaker. Then, put on your warm socks and sweatpants, and relax.

Quick Tips for Handling Q and A

1. Repeat the question. Audience members may have difficulty hearing one another.
2. Keep a pen and note card at the podium so you can jot down questions with multiple parts. That way you will be sure to respond to the entire question.
3. Don't be afraid to tell the audience, "I don't know," if you don't. This is a better option than guessing or giving out wrong information. Point the audience member to resources for more information when possible.
4. Don't fight back. Some audience members may try to challenge the speaker, play devil's advocate, or simply express strong opinions that are in opposition to your own. Don't raise your voice or become verbally combative. Acknowledge and thank the speaker for his or her point of view.
5. Address the entire audience. Frequently audience members ask questions about their own personal situations. Use the questions as a springboard to address themes that would be of interest to the audience as a whole.
6. Keep it moving. Often, the speaker responds to the first question with a long answer, and the balance of give and take between the speaker and the audience (one of the benefits of a question-and-answer session) is destroyed. So, maintain a fairly brisk pace.
7. Keep your answers brief, and keep an eye on the clock for the entire session. Prolonged question-and-answer sessions, unless built into the program, can become tedious, as audience members will have varying degrees of interest in your topic and different motivations for being in the audience.

CHAPTER FOUR

Tools of the Trade: Delivery Resources

In 1931, before the invention of television had reached the population at large, the *New York Times* reported that First Lady Lou Hoover had set up a "small improvised laboratory" in the White House. Apparently, she sought to improve her speaking voice for "appearances before sound picture cameras" ("Mrs. Hoover," 1931, p. 4). Mrs. Hoover's concerns about communication technology appear to have been well founded. A speech professor who later examined tapes from her radio broadcasts judged her voice to be "tinny" and noted that early twentieth century broadcasting equipment was poorly adjusted for the female voice, since so few women of that time had access to radio. (Gutin, 1989, p. 49).

Another prominent woman speaker, upon approaching a microphone, asked, "Does this pick up women's voices?" (Dyson, 1999, p. 44). The problem is that the woman who asked this question was Ann Winblad, and the comment was made in the 1990s rather than in the 1930s. Ann Winblad is a software venture capitalist named by *Business Week* as one of the twenty-five elite power brokers in Silicon Valley. When we compare the Hoover and Winblad stories, it doesn't look like women speakers have accomplished much over the decades when it comes to using presentation technology.

Although Winblad's story may represent an extreme, there is no doubt that women and men approach technology differently. There is also no doubt that, as a public speaker, you will be required to use technology—something as simple as an overhead projector or something more complex like a PC interactive whiteboard. In this chapter, we will take a look at some of the challenges women face in using presentation tools. We are defining tools in the broadest possible sense: everything a speaker has at her disposal to enhance the public speaking experience, from microphones and multimedia to the English language itself. Before you continue, review the discussions on technology, visual aids, and language in your primary textbook.

Specifically, in this chapter, we will introduce you to some of the speaker's technological tools, and we'll examine some of the stereotypes about women and computers. We will also address microphones, television cameras, teleprompters, and other tools used in mediated situations. Finally, we will introduce you to the gender differences associated with what we consider a speaker's universal tool—language itself.

The World of Gendered Technology

Computers have revolutionized the way we do business, yet stereotypes persist when it comes to gender and technology. Is technology still a man's world? Are women more reticent about using a microphone and other audiovisual equipment? Are women less likely to tinker with computers and, therefore, less likely to spend time creating a handout with presentation software? Researchers Ogletree and Williams (1990) cited numerous studies portraying males as having more favorable attitudes towards computers, using computers more than females, and perceiving themselves as more competent than females when it comes to computers. In 1997, Whitley conducted a meta-analysis of over eighty-two previous studies and found that men and boys have more positive attitudes and computer self-efficacy than women and girls. In a cross-cultural study, Reinen and Plomp (1997) found that girls in a number of countries "knew less about information technology than male students, enjoyed using computers less and perceived more problems with software" (p. 65).

Keogh and her colleagues (2000) designed a study in which thirteen- and fourteen-year-olds, in mixed and same gender pairs, were asked to examine a poem that had been scrambled and then put the lines back in order. In one variation, the poem was presented on paper, and students used scissors to cut the lines and move them around into a satisfactory order. Two weeks later, students were asked to examine another poem and rearrange the lines using a computer. When working with the poem on paper, there were no noticeable differences between the mixed and same gender pairs in terms of verbal or physical interaction (who controlled the scissors or manipulated the paper strips, for example). But with the computer version, things were different. In mixed gender pairs, boys spoke up more, made more proposals, argued more, and controlled the mouse more than when they were in same gender pairs. Girls were just the opposite. In mixed gender pairs, they spoke up less often and had less control of the mouse.

Apparently, the differences experienced by thirteen- and fourteen-year-olds also shows up in college classrooms. Brosnan (1998) reported that undergraduate females had more anxiety than undergraduate males when it came to computers, and 64 percent of the females agreed that computing was a male activity. Is it possible that these attitudes develop with the help of teachers' stereotyped behaviors?

GIRLS ARE UNDERREPRESENTED IN COMPUTER SCIENCE CLASSES

The Washington Post reported that boys outnumber girls three to one in computer science courses at high schools in Fairfax County, Virginia. The newspaper article referred to these high tech classes as the new "boys clubs." Alarmingly, the statistics from Fairfax County mirror national trends. Why don't girls take computer classes? For one thing, children's computer games are male dominated and don't speak to the interests of girls. Further, teachers direct girls toward word processing as the only computer skill needed. Unless school districts reverse this trend, women will be unprepared to work and communicate appropriately in an increasingly high tech workplace.

(Source: Victoria Benning (1998, July 14). Gender Gap in Fairfax Computer Classes. *The Washington Post*, B1, B5.)

Examine the situation presented in the box below and see what you think. Note that there are reports (AAUW, 2000) that women make up only 20 percent of the information technology workforce, and participation in such career paths has actually been decreasing over time.

Do such gender differences like the ones we are discussing play out when it comes to presentation technology? A study (Bauer, 2000) of female pre-service teachers may shed some light on this question. Pre-service teachers are in their last semester of college, and they teach during the day. Teachers are good subjects for technology studies because they not only help influence the attitudes of children about computers and other topics, but use computers and presentation technology on an almost daily basis. Based on a questionnaire distributed to the participants, Bauer found that 85 percent thought men knew more about technology, and 86 percent thought men were better able to solve a complex computer problem. Of those studied, 60 percent said they could create and use a Microsoft PowerPoint presentation, one of the most common presentation technology tools. The pre-service teachers study corresponds with results obtained from the business world. In a cross-cultural study of business people in the United States and Sweden, researchers found that men give more electronic presentations than women (Griffin, Pettersson, & Johnson, 1997).

Popular culture plays some part in creating these disparate images. For example, a study by Steinke and Long (1995) of children's science programs on television, including *Bill Nye The Science Guy*, *Beakman's World*, *Newton's Apple*, and *Wizard's World*, found that not only were there more male scientists portrayed, but females generally played supportive roles like science reporters and laboratory assistants. Another study by Morse and Daiute (1992) reported that men appear in advertisements in popular computer magazines significantly more often than women do.

Even Barbie has been caught up in the stereotype. In the fall of 1999, Mattel released the Barbie PC. Pink and priced at about $600, the computer comes loaded with software. However, the corresponding computer for boys, Hot Wheels PC, comes with twice the amount of software. The Hot Wheels PC includes a program about human anatomy and an educational game called *Logical Journey of the Zoombinis*. Mattel denies any gender bias and told the *New York Times* (Headlam, 2000) that some of the more popular Barbie software, like *Barbie Fashion Designer* and *Detective Barbie*, simply take up more room.

If the stereotypes are true, then we might conclude that women are less likely to use some of the new software available for creating visual aids or less willing to develop presentations that involve the operation of projection equipment. Morse and Daiute (1992) suggest that the stereotypes are not true, but rather that males and females approach computers differently. Just as there are masculine and feminine styles of communicating, there may be masculine and feminine approaches to the use of computers and technology.

Communication expert Deborah Tannen observed that "most women (with plenty of exceptions) aren't excited by tinkering with the technology, grappling with the challenge of eliminating bugs or getting the biggest and best computer" (1994, p. 53). In other words, she suggests that women simply want the computer to work. Men, on the other hand, enjoy getting the machine to perform. A male colleague of Tannen's described helping another man with a computer problem: "I once installed a hard drive for a guy, and he wanted to be there with me, wielding the screwdriver." Tannen's colleague went on to say that, in contrast, women "just want [me] to get the computer to the point where they can do what they want" (p. 53).

Sherry Turkle, a well-known social scientist who has extensively studied the relationship between people and technology, makes similar observations. We were particularly struck by this passage from Turkle's highly acclaimed book *Second Self* (1984) in which she wrote about her observations of children learning the LOGO computer language:

> Hard mastery is the imposition of will over the machine through implementation of a plan. A program is the instrument of premeditated control. Getting the program to work is more like getting "to say one's piece" than allowing ideas to emerge in the give-and-take of conversation ... The goal is always getting the program to realize the plan.
>
> Soft mastery is more interactive ... the mastery of the artist: try this, wait for a response, try something else, let the overall

shape emerge from an interaction with the medium. It is more like a conversation than a monologue. (p. 104)

The comparison of hard mastery to soft mastery bears a striking resemblance to the feminine and masculine styles of communication we discuss in Chapter One, and Turkle herself notes that hard masters tend to be male, soft masters tend to be female. She continues, "There are many reasons why we are not surprised that girls tend to be soft masters. In our culture girls are taught the characteristics of soft mastery—negotiation, compromise, give-and-take—as psychological virtues, while models of male behavior stress decisiveness and the imposition of will" (p. 109). Earlier, we similarly described the masculine style of rhetoric as one in which the speaker commands respect and attention—similar to a monologue. In contrast, the feminine style emphasizes relationship building with the audience—similar to a conversation.

Paul Edwards, building upon Turkle's work, writes that in our culture "computers, scientists, and men are hard; children, nurses and women are soft . . . In practice of course the image is totally false . . . neither men nor experts in formal thinking hold a monopoly on scientific abilities. Women are fully capable of all of the tasks of science and computer work. Equally, men have their own kinds of softness and intuition" (1990, p. 104).

So, just as a feminine-style speaker may have a different approach to organizing and delivering a speech, she (or he) may have a different approach to creating visual aids and using technology in a presentation. We encourage you, therefore, to experiment with the technology available to you (see the note on presentation software in the box below) or to learn more through the many publications and courses devoted to computers. Professor Bodenheimer, for example, took just one course in HyperCard (a Macintosh product and one of the earliest multimedia software programs) in graduate school and developed a basic set of skills that can still be applied to many of the newer presentation programs. Furthermore, I found the tinkering I had to do to complete my homework assignments a much needed creative outlet amidst the more traditional papers and library research required for other courses.

PRESENTATION SOFTWARE

Presentation software comes with most of the popular office software suites. A suite is a group of software products that are linked together. For example, Microsoft Office, the most popular of the current office software suites with a 90 percent share of the market, contains Word (word processing), Excel (spreadsheet), Access (database), Outlook (email and scheduling), and PowerPoint (presentations). PowerPoint gives you the ability to generate slides, overheads, and handouts for any public presentation you might be making. Other best-selling presentation software includes Lotus Freelance Graphics and Corel Presentations. Go to a local retail store or shop online to find out more about what's compatible with your computer and price range.

(Source: Bernard Simon. (2002, August 29). WordPerfect Gets New Life in Deal With 2 PC Makers, *The New York Times*, 5.)

Getting Equipped

Traditional or High Tech?

However you use computers, you cannot deny that computer technology has entered nearly every aspect of your life, and giving speeches is no exception. A recent television commercial showed a woman wearing fuzzy bunny slippers and using her home computer to conduct a high-level meeting. You, too, can sit on the beach, at your favorite coffee shop, or at your desk and create a professional slide presentation with the click of a mouse. Later, you can display that same presentation in a big auditorium for an audience to see.

In the late 1990s, worldwide sales of LCD (liquid crystal display) and DLP (digital light processing) projectors grew significantly—almost 70 percent in 1997 and another 40 percent in 1998 (Heimes, 1997a, 1997b). Millions of copies of Microsoft Office have been sold in the United States, and each contains the popular software PowerPoint for making slides and handouts.

Although this chapter is in no way intended to be a comprehensive technology guide, we think you should be aware of some of the new options available for clarifying or enhancing your message. At the very least you ought to know what others can and are doing so you do not appear to be hopelessly behind the times. For a long time, we assumed technology was something "other" people used—that is, until the day Professor Bodenheimer was explaining how to best use a flipchart and easel during a presentation skills workshop, and a participant raised her hand to politely ask about using her LCD panel. Of course, just having the technology available does not mean you have to use it. Sometimes a simple flipchart is exactly the right tool, and in the next section we provide you with some tips for effectively using the speaker's more traditional equipment. Let us emphasize this point: appropriate technology (high or low) should be matched with the purposes or needs of your speech. As you read the next few pages, we hope you'll keep in mind that the content of your presentation should drive your use of the technology, and not the other way around. While colored markers and dancing bullet points are fun and functional, they cannot substitute for well-researched, coherent, and thoughtful content.

Traditional Tools

Even with the multitude of multimedia tools available, the overhead projector is still the favorite of many presenters. Some experts believe that the slides created on computers are only better in terms of cosmetics and not worth the cost. Others suggest that taking technology-driven presentations on the road is begging for disaster. In contrast, one could argue that overhead projectors and transparencies are rather outdated, considering all of the possibilities computers present for getting one's message across. Still, the overhead projector is readily available in most auditoriums, most hotel meeting rooms, and the classroom down the hall. The overhead projector also has the added advantage of being relatively inexpensive.

These days, you might also find yourself using a visual presenter. Although the visual presenter looks like an overhead projector, it is a modern twist on the traditional equipment. With the visual presenter, you can place a page from a book or a piece of paper directly on the machine. The step of making a transparency is eliminated. You can also place a 3-D object on the machine and project and magnify it for your audience.

Flipcharts are the other favorite traditional visual tool. Flipcharts are just right for a small training workshop. We recommend the chapter in Clella Jaffe's *Public Speaking: A Cultural Perspective* (2001) entitled "Visual Aids: From Chalkboard to Computer" as a place to find technical tips on executing presentations using overhead projectors and flipcharts.

Two gender-related points are useful when learning to use these common presentation tools. Professor Bodenheimer was recording participants' answers to a discussion question on a transparency one day when I realized the suit I was wearing (a skirt and stand-alone jacket with no blouse) might be revealing more than I wanted to share as I leaned over the machine. Luckily, a flipchart was nearby, and I switched to that tool as soon as I gracefully could. Speaking of flipcharts, since many women are under five feet, four inches in height, and since short skirts are popular again, we suggest that you reach up to turn to a fresh page on the flipchart before the audience arrives. Also be careful when pulling down a projection screen or writing on the chalkboard.

Technological Tools

Most computers now include presentation software, which we mentioned earlier in this chapter. This software allows you to create your own handouts, including professional graphs and charts. In addition, with many programs, a speaker can create electronic slide shows with low level animation, or, as Hanke describes it, "text motion" (1997, p. 55). With this kind of animation, you can reveal one bullet point at a time as you discuss it or electronically underline a key point. Using multimedia software, one can create even more visually sophisticated presentations with sound, video clips, animation, and nonlinear interaction among the participants, the facilitator, and the medium—an advantage for trainers coaching participants at different skill levels, as each individual can work at her own pace and in the order that she chooses.

The proliferation of PowerPoint, in particular, may have some drawbacks, and users have been debating the usefulness of this software for at least seven years. Professor Bodenheimer is a subscriber to trdev@yahoogroups.com (formerly TRDEV-L), a listserv discussion group for professionals in the field of training and development. (A listserv is an internet forum, usually devoted to a particular topic. To learn more about the training and development discussion group, visit http://groups.yahoo.com/group/trdev/.) In the mid-1990s, training professionals in this group complained that PowerPoint and similar presentations were everywhere—the same clip art, the same basic slide formats. As a result, the presentations no longer had the same impact because the slides were becoming cliche. Another subscriber complained that one could not write on a slide or change a software presentation if feedback or discussion from the audience warranted such a change. Today, PowerPoint does include an onscreen pen, which is used by moving the mouse, although it requires a steady hand.

The controversy over PowerPoint continues. In 1997, Scott McNealy, CEO of Sun Microsystems banned PowerPoint at his company, suggesting that employees were spending too much time creating slick slides and not enough time developing their ideas (Maney, 1999). Similarly, General Hugh Shelton, former Chair of the Joint Chiefs of Staff, urged military personnel to keep their presentations simple (Jaffe, 2000).

Women need to be aware of the controversy over this popular way of giving presentations. If your workplace is like Sun Microsystems or the military, using PowerPoint could damage your credibility. On the other hand, not using PowerPoint could hurt your reputation. Katherine Hutt, the owner of a public relations firm, told *Presentations* magazine: "You almost wonder now when you walk into a presentation and someone *doesn't* use PowerPoint. You want to ask them, 'Are you from the Dark Ages?'" (Ganzel, 2000, p. 55). There are also good old-fashioned gender stereotypes still at play. Recently, Professor Natalle was assisting a guest lecturer with his presentation by handling the PowerPoint slides from a console while the guest stood before an audience in a large auditorium. With photographs and other graphics included, some of the software was slow to load, causing a short delay in the next display. Additionally, the speaker had his back to me so that I could not read his cues with 100 percent accuracy. As a result, I went to the next slide too soon at several points in the lecture. True to stereotype, my (male) boss sent a secretary to the front of the auditorium to ask me if I needed help. My guess is that if a man had been assisting, my boss would not have presumed help was needed. I felt like my credibility was damaged in front of some of my peers and students. Because credibility continues to be a concern for many women who present in public, learning what is appropriate and expected in your field could be critical to your success. You may also want to prepare a comeback when a man asks you if you are afraid of technology.

Of course, as we stated earlier, this brief overview is in no way intended to be a comprehensive guide to presentation technology, but rather an introduction to the possibilities. While you may decide an overhead projector is just the right thing, you should know that computers and LCD projectors are increasingly more common. As you look ahead to your next presentation, you may want to consider incorporating something new—perhaps starting with something as simple as a laser pointer. Whichever equipment you select, don't forget to practice, practice, practice.

Microphones

We can tell you unequivocally, after more than twenty years of professionally observing public speakers, that using a microphone is one of the biggest technical problems speakers encounter. Let us repeat that: Using a microphone is one of the biggest technical problems speakers encounter. Yet, most public speakers will need to use either a lavaliere (also called a clip-on) or stationary microphone sooner or later. A lavaliere microphone clips onto your lapel; a stationary microphone rests on a stand, although some can convert into a handheld version. A microphone helps your voice reach the far corners of the room. On our own, many of us do not (or cannot) project our voices as far as we think we do (or would like to).

A study by Debra Hansen and Sheri Irvin (1996), of San Jose State University, suggests that women are more timid about microphone use than men. In an interactive video course where students participated in class discussions in "real time" from several hundred miles away, Dr. Hansen found that microphones gave students the biggest problems, compared to other technical equipment such as cameras and monitors. She wrote: "Students, especially at the distant site, had to be assertive to make their questions heard. Male students appeared more comfortable with this arrangement and became the primary discussants. Many women refused to use the microphone, to have their voices broadcast or their ideas recorded on videotape. As a result, traditional female reticence silenced many women" (p. 14). As a graduate student in the class, Sheri Irvin observed: "I have participated in three interactive video classes and witnessed the reactions of other women students. Most were not comfortable with distance education . . . they worried over technical and equipment problems, such as using microphones and being televised when speaking in class" (p. 14).

Lavaliere microphones, in particular, have eliminated some of the technical hassle of using a microphone, but unfortunately, a speaker often finds herself behind a stationary microphone, which will be either attached to a lectern or free standing on the stage. Most speakers groan at the thought of being restricted behind a stationary microphone, so always ask for a lavaliere, or clip-on, microphone if you can request equipment. Think ahead about what to wear. You will need to have a lapel or collar for attaching the lavaliere microphone. Avoid tight fitting clothing so you can slip the transmitter in a pocket or clip it onto your waistband under a jacket. Place the microphone no higher than lapel level and avoid layered clothes that swish or move. The audio is best when unimpeded by complicated clothing.

One of the ways to make a microphone perform as an extension of your voice is to learn to listen to your speech while you are using the microphone. You will sound different than when your voice is not being amplified, and those differences are crucial to the success of your presentation. With a microphone, the sound is delayed, and certain sounds, like "s," are enhanced. You must listen to your pacing so that you can deliver the words at a rate that works with the delay over the sound system. And since you don't want to sound like a snake hissing, practice the "s" sound so that you don't slur or draw the sound out too long.

In addition, inexperienced speakers sometimes unintentionally cause the sound system to produce screeching feedback or muffled "ppppp" sounds. Other speakers, resenting having a piece of equipment in their faces, work against the microphone, rather than letting it act as a necessary extension of their voices. Avoiding these mistakes will take practice, so you might want to arrange some time with a speech coach or arrive early and practice your speech with the microphone on.

Here are a few simple guidelines for using a microphone effectively:

1. Do not test the microphone in front of the audience; check out the equipment before the audience arrives. Never blow into the microphone or bang on it with your fingers. Don't wait until you start speaking and then interrupt yourself by asking the audience, "Can you hear me?"
2. Speak using your normal pitch and volume—the microphone will do the rest.
3. Aim a hand-held microphone toward your mouth (versus under your chin).
4. Keep the microphone about six to eight inches away from your mouth.
5. If you will be wearing a lavaliere microphone, a suit is best; the microphone can be clipped onto your suit front, and the transmitter can be clipped onto your waistband, underneath your jacket, or slipped into your pocket.
6. A stationary microphone allows the speaker some flexibility for movement—you can turn your head from side to side—but learn its range before you begin your presentation.
7. Do not clink a microphone with rings or bracelets, put a microphone down on a hard surface, or rustle paper or notes in front of it.
8. Find the on/off switch and use it after you finish speaking, so that you do not inadvertently speak to other guests and have those personal remarks amplified all over the auditorium.

The Tools of Mass Media

If you are asked to speak via a television camera, you will probably find yourself in a television studio with a lavaliere microphone pinned to your jacket and heavier makeup than normal. You will also be sweating under the hot studio lights and looking into a teleprompter, while a floor director is giving you cues. We have already talked about microphones. Speaking to a television camera while reading off a teleprompter is another unique experience, and it takes a fair amount of practice to do it effectively. Some years ago, Professor Natalle was asked to make a training video in which I was to serve as the academic expert on sexual harassment. It was my first opportunity to speak in a television studio. The director, Tim Barkley, taught me a number of useful techniques such as maintaining an evenly pitched vocal register; looking directly into the camera as if in conversation with a friend; and keeping shoulder muscles relaxed so that upper body and head movements are natural rather than stiff.

As I prepared to work on this chapter of the handbook, I revisited my colleague and asked him what he knew about women's behavior in the studio. Tim shared with me many useful observations that allowed me to compare my own behavior in front of a camera. Generally, women are more likely than men to begin a taping session by berating their looks and ability in front of a TV camera. In other words, they denigrate their speaking skills and complain that they will look fat on camera. I recall being overly critical, myself, when I taped the sexual harassment video. I also recall that I fell into the trap of letting my voice reach an unnaturally high pitch as a result of my nervousness. How can you change your attitude and mind-set before stepping in front of a camera? First, recognize the fact that everyone looks about ten pounds heavier on camera. If this is a problem for you, and you are going to speak frequently on television, then think about losing ten pounds or ask the producer for suggestions on a wardrobe that has slimming effects. Second, calm down. The only people in the studio are usually the floor director and the camera operators, unless you have some fellow panelists with you. There is no reason to be afraid of a camera. See it as an opportunity to look good in front of an audience.

What happens when you need to read your lines or a speech from a teleprompter? Again, there are a few simple techniques that will help you use this tool effectively. The camera and the teleprompter are one device. As you look at the prompter, you will see your own words, and they will roll along at the same pace as you are speaking. If you speed up, the teleprompter operator (who is usually working in another room in the studio) will speed up. The teleprompter operator is a trained professional who is keeping up with you, so you set the pace. If you find yourself going too fast, simply slow down. Focus your eyes on the upper third of the words, and stay there. The text will scroll along so that you shouldn't have to move your head up and down. To avoid giving the audience the impression that you are reading, move your head slightly from side to side as if you were in natural conversation. Watch a professional news commentator, and you can see these techniques in action. Talk to the camera as if you were talking to a friend, and use vocal inflection and pauses just like natural conversation. In a short time, you should be able to learn these skills. There is nothing difficult about being on television when the focus is on you as a single speaker.

There are, however, more complications when you are on live television with a panel of speakers or in an interview situation. In this kind of speaking situation, you must learn to take cues from a moderator or interviewer and, perhaps, from a floor director who may be cueing you as well. Fear not! Rehearsal time is usually built into this type of speaking. As you are learning presentation techniques in a studio, ask to see a copy of the technical rehearsal videotape so that you can engage in some constructive criticism of your skills. If you are wondering about your personal appearance, there will be makeup artists to assist you. There are also do's and don'ts regarding dress, such as stay away from flashy jewelry that might reflect studio lights. Wear solid colors rather than plaids so that you stand out from backdrops without looking like you are swimming in patterns. Again, you will receive coaching and assistance in the studio, so our discussion here is simply to acquaint you with some general techniques and considerations regarding tools in mediated speaking situations.

An interview situation can be highly enjoyable or a disaster, and much depends upon the rapport you build with the interviewer. When the questions are interesting and create a back-and-forth type of interaction, you will find yourself feeling like you are in the middle of a good conversation rather than engaging in public speaking. Nevertheless, the same kinds of considerations just discussed still need to be attended to in your delivery. There may be a teleprompter, behind or to the side of the interviewer, that you must read from if your responses are scripted. Be prepared to sit close to the interviewer (knees almost touching). If you bring note cards to the interview, they should be blue and no larger than four by six inches. White index cards reflect light and large cards get in the way. The best thing you can do in an interview is answer sincerely and completely, and enjoy yourself. Rely on the interviewer to use her or his skills to guide both of you through the communication experience.

Language

In thinking and talking about the many tools of the public speaker, our discussions always returned to language itself. Although we use language every day—and it is an, if not the, essential part of every communication act—most of us don't think much about it. Language is a wondrous gift. Each individual can mold and shape language to create unique and sensational special effects without pressing a single key on the computer. The words you select and the way you put them together are powerful tools for creating a vivid image or feeling for your audience.

Language can also harm your relationship with the audience, and many speakers have unintentionally foiled their message by using terms that others have found offensive.

A polished, sensitive, and effective trainer, with whom we sometimes work, once gave out an assignment for workshop participants to complete over lunch. Knowing that work over lunch isn't always a popular option, she tried to lighten the moment with a bit of dry humor and said, "Now, I am afraid I have to be a bit of a slave master. I have an assignment for you to complete during lunch." Later, one of the participants suggested that the term *slave master* was offensive, given that a majority of the participants were African American. Although some might consider the participant to be overly sensitive, this case illustrates the power of language—for that participant, just two words damaged the rapport the speaker had worked so hard to build all morning.

Still, language isn't something to be feared. Use language to convey your ideas with passion and precision. Spend a little extra time selecting words so you can create a specific mood or feeling for the listeners. Language is the tool that can make the difference between a good and a great speech. There is a connection between gender, language, and audience perception of the speaker. We want to spend some time explaining this connection because it is crucial to the choices you will make in selecting the most effective language for your message.

The Gender-Linked Language Effect

Anthony Mulac and a team of researchers (1998) at the University of California at Santa Barbara have been studying the linguistic characteristics of speech used by male and female speakers. After more than fifteen years of research, Mulac has found that language is indeed different for women and men, and that audiences do judge speakers differently based on language alone. His theory is called "The Gender-Linked Language Effect." He has identified consistent differences in linguistic features that have an effect on the audience's judgment of the speaker. The male features of speech, according to Mulac, are references to quantity ("80 percent of the time"), first person singular pronouns ("I"), elliptical sentences ("Beautiful!"), directives ("Let's do it like this."), locatives ("sitting next to the . . ."), and judgmental adjectives ("the best way," "a poor choice"). The female features of speech are adverbials beginning a sentence ("During the 1990s, many women found . . ."), oppositions ("You should have prepared the agenda, but perhaps it could have waited until later."), questions ("What should the proposal contain?"), references to emotions ("I'm so happy . . ."), intensive adverbs ("That's very nice."), dependent clauses (". . . which is designed with . . ."), mean length sentences (defined as the number of words per sentence), uncertainty verbs ("I'm not sure . . ."), negations ("You don't want to go."), and hedges ("sort of").

What judgments do audiences make? Males are consistently perceived as dynamic (strong and aggressive speech), while female speakers are seen as aesthetic (nice and beautiful speech) and high on sociointellectual status (speech reflecting high social status and literacy). For our purposes, what is interesting about Mulac's research is the important questions that it raises for female speakers. What do these perceptions mean? Does a feminine style work with audiences? What is power as reflected in a speaker's language? How are gender-linked styles of speaking effective in reaching goals? Although we do not have the answers to all these questions, research such as this provides increasingly precise insight into ourselves as public speakers.

Gendered Humor

Humor is a dimension of language that contains definite gender differences. A joke is a great way to start a speech—if it works. And, in fact, there are many funny women who have used one-liners, wit, and jokes to great advantage in their public speaking and writing—Gloria Steinem, Rita Mae Brown, Ellen Goodman, Maureen Dowd, and Whoopi Goldberg come to mind. However, and we are sending up a big red flag here, using humor is chancy, especially if you are not good at executing it. As we mentioned in Chapter Two, many speech trainers insist that every speech should start with a joke, but our experience tells us that jokes are not always the best choice. For one thing, what is funny to you may not be funny to your audience. Furthermore, a joke that the audience does not get or does not think is funny is equivalent to pulling a fire alarm—your audience will, at least psychologically, run out the door. You are also likely to lose credibility because the audience may conclude that you haven't done your homework or that you can't relate to them.

There is some credible evidence that women and men use humor differently and have different comfort levels with telling jokes. For example, women tend to make themselves the butt of the joke (see the Hillary Clinton discussion below), while men more often use someone else as the target of the joke (Barreca, 1991). Further, it appears that men are more practiced and comfortable in telling funny stories and leading up to a punch line than women. Language researcher Mary Crawford (1995) found that men use more hostile humor and formulaic joke telling, while women prefer anecdotes and stories. Finally, men and women often find different things to be funny; for example, men often enjoy sexual humor more than women. Make a note in the margin of this page regarding your own comfort level with humor.

In the example below, Hillary Rodham Clinton uses humor to tastefully make fun of herself. She also refers to the Chicago setting for the 1996 Democratic Convention, where this speech is taking place. Since Clinton is a Chicago native, this reference to the setting helps her establish an especially strong rapport with the audience, as does her mention of one of Chicago's outspoken star basketball players, Dennis Rodman. In addition, she references a current event. At the time of the convention, a child had fallen into the gorilla area at a local zoo, but was miraculously moved out of harm's way by a female gorilla. The gorilla story was covered by local and national news media.

> I have so many friends here, people who have been important to me all my life, and it seems like every single one of them has given me advice on this speech. One friend suggested that I appear here with Binti, the child-saving gorilla from the Brookfield Zoo. You know, as this friend explained, Binti is a typical Chicagoan, tough on the outside, but with a heart of gold underneath. Another friend advised me that I should cut my hair and color it orange and then change my name to Hillary Rodman Clinton.

Qualifiers and Tag Questions

Communication professors Kearney and Plax (1999) suggest eliminating qualifying phrases like "I know this may not sound right, but" and "I'm not sure, but." Similarly, phrases like "I am not an expert, but" or "I hope this helps" may be perceived as weak and characteristic of a speaker who is unsure of herself. In a study of decision making in small groups, Bradley (1981) found that women who used qualifiers and tag questions ("That's a good idea, isn't it?") were perceived as less dynamic, less knowledgeable, and less intelligent than women who did not use those devices in expressing their views. When men used tag questions or qualifiers, there was no significant difference in the perception of the men's dynamism, knowledge, or intelligence. In similar studies, Linda Carli found that tentative speech actually helped women to influence male listeners, but reduced a woman speaker's ability to influence another woman. Carli continues, "Moreover, both male and female speakers judged a woman who spoke tentatively to be less competent and knowledgeable than a woman who spoke assertively, but did not consider language when rating the competence and knowledge of male speakers" (1990, p. 946). Although one would not normally expect someone who is not competent or knowledgeable to be influential, the research suggests that a woman may use the tentative style strategically, specifically to demonstrate to male audience members that she is not stepping on their toes or trying to gain status in the social hierarchy. In general, however, we recommend avoiding a tentative style, unless using it strategically with a male audience for which social status may be a factor.

Hopeless

Although every speaker must develop her own style, there is one phrase we urge you to avoid, the infamous *I hope*, sometimes disguised as *hopefully*: "I hope I have enlightened you today," "I hope you'll bear with me—I have a bit of a cold," or "Hopefully, in the future we will all live together in peace." *I hope* makes the speaker sound weak and wishy-washy. Women tend to use this approach more than men. Contrast the following two sentences:

With your donations, I hope we will find a cure for cancer.
With your donations, I know we will find a cure for cancer.

The second sentence is clearly stronger and more likely to achieve the desired effect.

Neutral Language

We believe in the importance of being sensitive to your audience; however, by suggesting the use of neutral language, we are not recommending a strict diet of politically correct terminology. Terms like *hair-challenged* (for bald men) or *job-deficient* (for the unemployed) are evasive and may backfire on the speaker. What we do recommend is that women be conscious of gender-biased language. It is easy to use such language without even realizing it. Use inclusive words like *postal worker, server, flight attendant,* and *spokesperson* instead of words that call unnecessary attention to one's gender such as *postman, waitress, stewardess,* or *spokesman*. Audiences today are much more sensitive to word endings and pronouns that indicate male bias, and research indicates that when people hear words like *postman,* they visualize a man. Whenever possible, use neutral forms of language (*people* rather than *mankind*) or inclusive forms of phrasing (*men and women* rather than *men*). Recently, Professor Bodenheimer heard a radio commentary about changes in the health care industry. Unfortunately, the commentator used the pronoun *she* when referring to nurse practitioners. He also made repeated references to his own physician, who just happened to be a man, and left the listener with the impression that physicians are men and nurse practitioners are women. There are male nurses, of course, as well as female doctors and auto mechanics. The language you use should include all.

Remember, tools are the key to a polished presentation and the revelation of you as a speaker. Some tools, such as language, are already at your disposal and need only fine tuning. Other tools, such as microphones and computers, are not as accessible. You will need to become familiar with their use before you can incorporate them into your public speaking in an effective manner. Over time, experience will make their use seem like second nature.

AVOIDING VERBAL VAGUENESS

We rarely conduct a public speaking workshop without someone asking how to control the unwanted "ums." *Um*, *like*, and *you know*, called verbal fillers, are meaningless, and young women often learn these speech patterns in their teenage peer group. If you lose your train of thought, instead of saying *um*, simply pause and collect your thoughts—it may seem like an eternity to you, but your audience will prefer those few seconds of silence over the annoying *um*. Similarly, *you know* and *like* (as in "I, like, disagree with the current policy, you know?") take up space without adding anything of value to your speech and give the impression of immaturity. Either you disagree with the policy or you don't.

We also suggest limiting the use of *very* ("She is very ill.") and *really* ("This is a really good proposal."). Because the terms are overused, it is hard to determine the speaker's exact meaning. In other words, how very is *very*? We recommend that you provide more specific information. For example, instead of simply saying that "she is very ill," you might provide the following statement: "She is seriously ill. The doctor says she is suffering from clogged arteries and may have had a minor stroke." Likewise, instead of simply saying that "this is a really good proposal," you might say that "this is a good proposal because it provides three specific steps for accomplishing the divisional goals."

CHAPTER FIVE

Public Speaking Situations

Sometimes we find ourselves speaking in public when we least expect it. First Lady Laura Bush suddenly found herself in the role of counselor and mourner after the devastation at the Pentagon and World Trade Center. In a *Washington Post* report (Gerhart, 2001), Mrs. Bush was described as "the one member of the administration who offers quiet words of reassurance and empathy, while the President and his key aides use the harsh rhetoric of war" (p. C1). The first lady almost certainly never envisioned a situation where her public speaking would actually involve eulogy or grief counseling, yet she did a superb job, by all assessments we have seen.

Although most of us are not as visible as Mrs. Bush, adult life affords many special situations where some sort of public speaking skill is required. This chapter focuses on some of the likely (and more happy) situations that require slightly different skills from the ones discussed in previous chapters, where we focused more on the contexts of traditional speech giving and training. Note that your primary textbook covers informative and persuasive speaking in depth. In this chapter, we begin with special occasions, discussing the speaking skills associated with making an introduction, giving or receiving an award, and offering a toast. We then talk a bit about sharing your expertise on a panel or as a moderator of a panel. Finally, we concentrate on workplace situations, where you may find yourself giving a report, handling a meeting, or training colleagues.

Special Occasions

Making an Introduction

As an active member of the community, you may be asked to introduce a keynote speaker or special guest, and this is usually considered an honor. Very often, you are introducing the speaker because you know this person or because you suggested this person as a speaker. If you know the person, that makes your job easier, but there is no reason not to give a good introduction even when you've never met the speaker. There are some specific components to an introduction, but you prepare and practice just like any other speech.

Your basic purposes in an introduction are to set up the audience for what to expect from the speaker and to make the speaker feel welcome. You ease the way and provide a level of comfort for the speaker so that she (or he) is positive and smiling by the time she reaches the podium. You create an atmosphere of receptivity and help the audience anticipate the content of the upcoming speech. You must do this within a short period of time (one to two minutes), so carefully select the most important facts and tidbits for the introduction. You must make sure to name the speaker, provide credentials or reasons for the speaker's presence at this event, and name the topic of the speech. There is not a set order for this content, and you may personalize the introduction as appropriate to your relationship with the speaker. A personal relationship often results in an introduction where a funny story or past event is relayed to the audience as part of complimenting the speaker. Just be sure you don't steal the speaker's thunder by telling something she or he is likely to use in her or his own introduction.

If you don't know the speaker, then your job may involve a little more research to prepare the introduction. You might need to see the speaker's resume or consult the books or articles this person has written. You can come up with a short, sincere introduction that will do nicely. Given that you don't know the speaker, it is imperative to check all your facts. Professor Bodenheimer was introduced once as a representative of Georgetown University when, in fact, she was from George Washington University. Speakers introducing people they don't know have a tendency to read the introduction, often stumbling and acting as if they are clueless. We have even seen speakers turn to the honored guest and verify items in the introduction. ("You did work for the Office of Health and Human Services, right?") Not only is such a mistake inconsiderate, it makes you look foolish and reduces your credibility.

You must prepare and practice an introduction regardless of how well you know the person you are responsible for introducing. Use your best interpersonal skills to act like you know what's happening and to show that you care. Professor Natalle once had an experience where a person handed her a two-page written introduction approximately five minutes before she was to introduce a panel of five speakers. There was simply no way to sound sincere reading something that I had no time to practice. To make matters worse, two panel members arrived late, which meant that the introduction got off to a late start. In this instance, I chose to ad-lib the introduction I had already prepared (which was accurate and appropriate) rather than try to master the material handed to me at the last minute.

We have included a sample introduction that was recently delivered at a women's studies conference to introduce a keynote speaker. The person giving the introduction is a quiet, unassuming professor of religious studies who does not consider herself a public speaker. Yet, after the introduction, and even later in the day, many people complimented Dr. Wakeman on her effective introduction. We offer here the power of ordinary, yet thoughtful, preparation.

> I am pleased and honored to introduce Katie Cannon, and eager, as I know you all are, to hear what she has to say, so my remarks will be brief.
>
> Dr. Cannon has done extensive work on the role of Black women in the Black church. In an interview, she said the biggest challenge of womanist moral discourse is to hold race, sex and class together—to think about them all at once. She said, "I come from a Black church tradition that says everything I am I owe back to the community. So my question always is, how do I bring with me the Black women's community of North Carolina to whom I

am accountable?" I admire the way she keeps her commitments to both the Black church and the academy, her community and her profession, without compromising either one. In fact, I don't know how she does it. I do know it takes much courage, moral integrity and deep faith, a strong sense of self, and a good sense of humor to continue to break down the barriers, to always be a front runner.

Katie is the first African-American woman to earn the Doctor of Philosophy degree from Union Theological Seminary in New York ('83) and the first African-American woman to be ordained to the ministry in the United Presbyterian Church in the USA ('74). Presently, she is Associate Professor of religion at Temple University, and has previously taught at Episcopal Divinity School in Cambridge. She has lectured widely, both here and abroad.

Dr. Cannon is the author of *Black Womanist Ethics* ('88), a founding work of African American Women's theology. In it, using Black women's novels as sacred texts, Dr. Cannon lays out a distinctive ethic of survival that challenges the basic assumptions of Eurocentric ethics.

Her new book ('95), *Katie's Canon: Womanism and the Soul of Black Community,* is a collection of her essays which cover a range of issues from biblical interpretation to the complex relationships between womanist and feminist scholars of religion. In her introduction to this book, Sara Lawrence-Lightfoot says, "Katie has a unique way of seeing, naming, critiquing, and analyzing her experience, a way of turning commonly held assumptions on their head. These essays are provocative, irreverent, strong. They rage. They provoke. They make us consider the privileges and impotence of our oppression and they challenge us to fight all forms of racism, sexism, classism, and homophobia."

Today, Katie Cannon is going to speak to us about "Catching Our Moral Breath: Womanist Methodology as a Mode of Transformative Action." So hang on to your seats! Now I want us to welcome Katie Cannon back home to North Carolina. (Wakeman, 1997)

When Professor Natalle asked Dr. Wakeman if we could include this introduction in our handbook, she was surprised. "But I'm not a public speaker," she protested. The introduction was written from Dr. Wakeman's experience reading Cannon's books, reviewing

Cannon's resume, and having a brief opportunity to meet Cannon the evening before the speech was given. The two women were not previously acquainted, yet the introduction is sincere and establishes the keynote speaker's credibility. By the end of the introduction, the audience was primed to hear the speech.

Giving or Receiving an Award

Giving and receiving awards are positive, and sometimes emotional, moments. Like introductions, the actual speaking time should be short and appropriate to the occasion. If you are giving an award, you should do two things: include information about the award being given and tell why the person receiving the award is deserving. More specifically, the essential information should include telling the purpose of the award and, if appropriate, some of the history surrounding the award. In announcing the recipient, you should say something about how that person met the criteria for earning the award. Here's how the speech would be structured:

> The Margaret Baker prize is awarded each year to an outstanding student in the Communication Department (information about the award being given). Margaret Baker was herself an outstanding communicator. She was the first woman ever to serve as a presidential speechwriter. She established this award at her alma mater to help young women entering the communication field (purpose and history of the award). Over thirty women apply for this award each year. A faculty panel selects a student who demonstrates excellence in her coursework, enthusiasm and growth in her internship, and active involvement in departmental or university co-curricular activities (criteria for selection). This year's recipient is Erica Johnson. Erica has maintained a 4.0 GPA for her entire junior year. She interned for twenty hours a week at the local CBS affiliate, where she recently was offered a job after graduation as a production coordinator. In addition, Erica actively served the Communication Club as vice president (recipient's qualifications).

As you call the person forward to receive the award, it is important to be in the best physical position for the presentation. Since there is usually a camera present, be sure that the award recipient is facing into the camera, and practice keeping your whole body as open to the audience and camera as possible when handing the award to the recipient. Practice your own comfort level with handing over a plaque and shaking hands at the same time. If you can't do both, then avoid the awkwardness by giving the plaque and then shaking hands. We have noted that there are some gender differences in how people congratulate award recipients. Women presenters often hug or kiss the recipient, but male presenters tend to shake hands with other males and hug or kiss female recipients. Do what is comfortable for you and appropriate for your relationship with the other person. Check the box below on women and hand shaking to see what you think about handshakes as a

---

MAKING AN IMPRESSION WITH A HANDSHAKE

Psychology professor William Chaplin and a team of researchers correlated hand shaking and personality characteristics of 112 college women. Women who were "more liberal, intellectual and open to new experiences" had firmer handshakes and made a more favorable impression on others. The study suggests a firm handshake may be a tool for women's self-promotion. This is a type of assertive business behavior where women are not penalized for behaving similar to men. Advice for women: Shake hands firmly to promote a favorable response.

(Source: William Chaplin, Jeffrey Phillips, Jonathan Clanton, Nancy Clanton, & Jennifer Stein. (2000). Handshaking, Gender, Personality and First Impression. *Journal of Personality and Social Psychology, 19,* 110–117.)

---

form of nonverbal impression management.

If you are the recipient of an award, you should say thank you in a sincere and humble manner. If there were important people who truly helped you earn that award, acknowledge them. The challenge here is to thank only those colleagues or intimates who really were instrumental in your winning, and avoid a laundry list of acknowledgments. We've all seen the Oscar winners who drone on and on only to be cut off by a commercial when their time is up. Recently, Professor Natalle was one of three recipients of an award given at her university. Each recipient was told that there would be time for a few words and to prepare some remarks. The first recipient came forward, gave an appropriate word of thanks, and sincerely related how her history as a former student at the university put her in a position that resulted in being tapped for the award. (I'd give her an A on this speech.) When the second recipient came forward, she opened a notebook and read a prepared speech that lasted over ten minutes and included a history of everyone who had been influential in her life since childhood. Meanwhile, her son was jumping around and running up to the podium as she spoke. Finally, she picked up her son and finished reading the speech to the last word. (This speech definitely earns a C.) I was the third recipient. Feeling some pressure from what had just transpired, and truly wanting to say only a few words, I abandoned my note card and gave an impromptu speech that essentially said how thrilled I was to receive the award and what a great place UNCG was to work. I related how my work in women's studies put me in position to nurture female students, in particular, thus resulting in the nomination for the award. (I'd give myself a B.) This experience taught me to pay better attention to my place in the lineup of speakers and to have two versions of an acceptance speech prepared: what I want to say and a really short version in case events turn out in some unexpected manner. Remember the Oscars.

Giving a Toast

Although there are various types of speeches that pay tribute to someone, giving a toast is the most common form. If you are asked in advance to give a toast, then you have time to think through what you want to say. A toast is a compliment in its sincerest form, so you should plan positive remarks that elevate the recipient to the highest level in the eyes of everyone in the room. Without being too emotional, praise the person's accomplishments and reinforce that everyone is at this occasion to help celebrate in the recipient's good fortune. We have noticed that women giving toasts sometimes cry, so try to stay dry-eyed long enough to get your words out. Also, avoid letting your pitch rise under the stress of emotion, and don't forget to project your voice if you are not in front of a microphone. Stay calm and enjoy yourself. A toast should be over in about thirty to forty seconds. If you are doing your job well, the recipient will be flattered, and the audience will be reinforced in their positive perceptions of the person just toasted. Take a look at this beautifully done toast to a bride and groom given by the bride's attendant:

> I think the best friendships are the ones that stand the test of time. Friends who love and accept you at your best and at your worst. Friends who are comfortable and fun to be with. Friends who challenge you to be the best you can be. I found such a friend in Katherine eleven years ago, and for that I will be forever grateful. Likewise, I believe the best marriages share the same characteristics: where love and acceptance come at the best and worst of times; where there is lots of laughter and fun; where you challenge each other to be the best you can be as individuals and as a couple; and where there is honesty even when it is hard. This is what I wish for Katherine and Jim, her new best friend. Please join me in a toast to Katherine and Jim and a lifetime of love, laughter, passion, and, most of all, friendship! (Fick-Cooper, 1997)

If you are called upon to give a speech for a special occasion that we have not mentioned here (for example, a eulogy), check your primary public speaking textbook. There will be instructions that are easy to follow. Now let's turn our attention to a different type of speaking situation.

Sharing Expertise on Panels

Often, you are called upon to participate in a public speaking event because of some expertise you possess. For example, you might be an expert in web design or PowerPoint, or you might be the president of a sorority that has done outstanding community service. The typical kinds of invitations you will receive include speaking at a meeting of a local organization, serving as a panel member for an educational forum, serving as a luncheon speaker for a club, acting as the moderator or chair in a town hall style discussion, or serving as an expert at a hearing. Most of the time people expect you to participate without any compensation, and they expect you to say "yes" to any and all invitations. Our first piece of advice is for you to decide how much community service you can do and whether or not you truly have the expertise for the situation at hand. Set out your own boundaries and learn to say "no" politely, but firmly. If you must turn down an invitation, try to suggest an alternative speaker so that you promote goodwill and leave the door open for future invitations. Also, if you do want an honorarium or speaker's fee, be prepared to ask for that up front as you negotiate the nature of the speaking situation. Women are sometimes shy about asking for money or negotiating a fee, but you should not be. If you need gas money or money to cover childcare expenses, then you will appreciate getting some remuneration for your time and contributions. Many organizations have sufficient funds to pay a token honorarium of twenty-five or fifty dollars.

If you are asked to serve on a panel of experts, prepare for this speaking situation by doing the same type of audience analysis and research that you read about earlier in this handbook. Find out from the contact person exactly what aspect of your expertise is needed so that you can focus your preparation on that area. A typical panel format is to have three to five panel members speak, each of whom gets about five to ten minutes presentation time, followed by a discussion with the audience. A key difference between this type of speaking and standing behind a podium as the featured speaker is that you share time with others, and you probably will be seated. There is a tremendous difference between speaking while sitting down and speaking while standing. Your movement is restricted, you must project your voice up and out a little better, and your view of the audience may be obscured in places. Practice this type of presentation if you have never done it before. Sit at your dining room table and visualize an audience in front of you. If you have participated on a panel, then you know that you must share time with others and be ready for a variety of questions from the audience. A good technique to develop as a panel member is to carefully listen to the other speakers so that you can refer to their points and relate them to your own presentation. Reinforcing, disagreeing, or clarifying the other panelists' points makes for a more coherent experience for everyone. A panel should be the culmination of the whole; that is, all the expertise should somehow dovetail by the time the panel discussion is over.

Sometimes you are tapped to be the panel moderator (also called the chair or facilitator). In fact, you should be practicing this skill in courses such as business communication and small group communication. If you are selected as a moderator, your job is to welcome the audience, introduce the panelists, keep track of the time, facilitate questions from the audience, and bring the panel to closure. This is no small task and takes some experience. We have both chaired panels where panel members would not stop talking, or where one panel member took up too much time giving long-winded answers to questions. The moderator might find it helpful to use five-by-eight-inch index cards with the words *2 minutes* and *STOP!* printed on them. If your panelists are not keeping an eye on the clock, you will have to use your flash cards to keep them posted. Don't be afraid to let panelists know their time is up, because the audience is counting on you to keep the program moving.

We have both served as panel moderators where we did not know the panel members. This presents a problem regarding introductions. Of course, you could select some items off an expert's resume to state along with the person's name and the company she or he works for, but there are more exciting ways to inject fun and create meaningfulness for the audience. Professor Natalle has developed a technique that works well. Before the panel begins, I approach each panel member as she or he arrives and introduce myself as the panel moderator. I welcome the panelist and say how much I appreciate their contribution of time and expertise. Then I ask a question: "Can you tell me one thing about your life or work experience that relates to what you have to say on today's panel?" I recently did this for a panel of women in media-related jobs who came to UNCG to share their professional advice with students getting ready to enter the job market. One panelist, who headed a local cable access TV station, told me that her first job out of college was as a cashier at a liquor store. As I introduced her, giving her credentials first, I said to the audience, "And Ms. X wants you to know that her first job out of college was at a liquor store." The audience laughed and wondered, "What on earth?" But the panelist made good use of this fact by talking about how the job turned into a management position that helped her build a resume. She was funny, credible, sharp, and an excellent role model for the students. Having that unexpected bit of information made for a successful presentation. Likewise, the other three panelists used the bit of information they'd given me to pump up their own presentations. We highly recommend trying a technique like this. We also recommend that you go back to the end of Chapter Three to review techniques for handling question-and-answer sessions since that will be a big part of your job as moderator.

Public Speaking in the Workplace

The workplace is the communication setting for numerous types of presentations, and many companies consider public speaking an important skill for employees. According to a study by the human resources firm of Goodrich and Sherwood (Petrin, 1993), candidates seeking management positions should have six essential skills: financial management, people management, writing, interviewing, public speaking, and training. We couldn't agree more. In fact, we have observed, albeit informally, that many of the participants who sign up for the various presentation workshops and public speaking classes we deliver are just as concerned about training workshops, briefings, and meetings as they are about formal speeches. In comparing notes with other colleagues who consult in business environments, we know that a large number of professionals simply are not trained in business speaking. Says public speaking professor James DiSanza (1998) of Idaho State University: "A relative of mine consults for a large Eastern manufacturer. She constantly complains about poor presentation skills demonstrated at one firm. She tells tales of informational 'briefings' that last three hours and claims that only people untrained in organizing their thoughts or analyzing an audience could think such practices appropriate." In the interest of work efficiency, there simply is no excuse for any company tolerating three-hour briefings. Everyone can speak well in the workplace with some basic information and practice.

There also seems to be a continuing belief that women may need to be better presenters than men in order to command attention and credibility in the workplace. *Presentations* magazine carried a series of articles on women as presenters in its August 1998 issue. As you might guess, the news had a familiar ring to it: women and men communicate using different stylistic features, and women are at a disadvantage

(Zielinski, 1998). Rather than dwell on this notion, we want to give you some assistance with the basics. We go back to our premise that preparation is the key to success. What we have said in previous chapters regarding gender considerations should be kept in mind as you read this chapter.

Giving a Report

The workplace situation most similar to giving a speech is delivering a report. Whether you are updating coworkers on the progress of a project or shareholders on finances, observe the same principles of public speaking outlined in earlier chapters. Our general advice about speaking extemporaneously holds true here too. Even if the audience members will be receiving a written version of the report, you should not simply read the report aloud because it will lower your credibility. In fact, if possible, we encourage you not to distribute written copies until your oral presentation is complete. Audience members will start flipping through the written version while you are speaking rather than listening to you. If for some reason you must distribute a written copy of the report, your job as speaker is to identify the highlights and then speak. (Notice we said "speak," and not "read.") Just as you would with a keynote address, develop an outline with an introduction, a body, and a conclusion, and then take time to practice. Your main points should mirror the main points of the written report, but your goal as a speaker is to discuss them, perhaps spicing your remarks with some interesting facts that are not included in the written version. Just as a cover letter highlights some of the accomplishments of an applicant not included in

PEANUTS reprinted by permission of United Feature Syndicate, Inc.

the formal resume, your presentation should entice the audience to read the written report for all the technical details.

When there is no written report to accompany the oral one, the same general rules for developing an outline and rehearsing still apply. Watch out for use of visual aids. We've seen too many presentations that are driven by graphs and slides. With all the new graphics software loaded onto our computers, report givers can easily get carried away with creating interesting slides. Unless the slides enhance or clarify a point, they are not necessary and may even distract the audience from focusing on your main ideas.

Meeting Mania

Even with the explosion of new communication devices—from the internet to cellular phones—we still spend an extraordinary amount of time in face-to-face meetings. A 1998 survey of twenty-eight hundred meeting participants and leaders, conducted by the 3M Meeting Network, found that most people spent a day to a day and a half per week in meetings. A similar survey, conducted by MCI WorldCom Conferencing, found that the typical professional goes to sixty meetings a month ("U.S. Businesses Pay," 1999). As a meeting participant or a meeting leader, you will be engaging in the most common form of public speaking, the impromptu speech. If you have ever responded to another's comments, made a suggestion, asked a question, or updated others on your own projects, you have already practiced impromptu speaking. Based on a survey of alumni at five different colleges and universities, communication scholars Johnson and Szczupakiewicz (1987) reported that impromptu speaking is the most important type of speech delivery in the business world.

When you speak at a meeting, your audience will not expect your remarks to be perfect. Nonetheless, take a few moments to jot down some notes if possible. Organize your thoughts around this simple pattern: introduce your idea and back it up with good reasons. For example: "I disagree with the proposal for two reasons. First, the market survey did not show strong enough support for such a product. Second, the expenses involved in launching a new product are considerable and our budget does not cover it." Notice here that the speaker got her point across and then yielded the floor to another. In other words, she did not ramble. We realize that not everything you want to express at a meeting fits neatly and succinctly into a few sentences, but a short and thoughtful answer is better than a long-winded monologue—something we've witnessed too many times at a meeting.

In addition, keep in mind that a descriptive, depersonalized style (rather than an evaluative, personal one) is always welcome in the communication setting of a meeting. For example, instead of saying, "Well, Mary, the report you wrote was lousy," try something like, "The report was a bit too long for publication in the newsletter." In the second example, the comment is about the report and not about Mary, and the speaker gives specific and constructive criticism.

If you are the meeting chair, your role will resemble the panel moderator role we described earlier in this chapter. You will share the spotlight with others, but maintain a structured format within a specific time period. Your job is to keep the meeting moving and make sure the comments made are relevant to the issue at hand. Some of the suggestions we made for handling question-and-answer sessions (see Chapter Three) apply here, so you may wish to review those techniques. And, just as a speaker must stay within the time limit, a meeting leader must make sure that the meeting starts and ends on time. Don't make those who arrived on time wait for others, and don't keep the meeting going beyond the agreed upon time limit. Suggest homework assignments if work still needs to be done beyond your time together. As the leader, your job includes guiding the group, so offer up your own opinion occasionally while letting other group members do most of the talking. You may need to concentrate on drawing out the opinions of quiet members while keeping the talkative members from dominating.

Training

Recently, Professor Bodenheimer went to see a play with a friend and colleague with whom she frequently conducts training. Shortly before the curtain rose, a woman tapped us on the shoulder and said, "Hey, aren't you the two women who conducted that workshop on cross-cultural communication?" In fact, the woman had attended a workshop my friend and I had taught at least a year earlier. She went on to say how much she enjoyed the class and commented that she not only learned, but had fun, especially in comparison to other workshops she had attended.

The positive feedback was bittersweet. Although my colleague and I were certainly appreciative of the compliments, we've heard all too often about those "other" workshops the theatergoer mentioned. Lecture driven and transparency saturated, too many training workshops follow the old classroom model: the teacher stands in front of the classroom and talks, while the participants sit in rows of chairs and listen. There is no interaction (and often no fun). Lectures are not inherently bad, and they certainly have their place, but there are many other effective tools available when the public speaking setting is the training workshop.

Every speech is interactive; that is, the speaker is always receiving nonverbal feedback from the audience. For training, however, interaction becomes more significant. While giving a speech, the spotlight is centered on the speaker on the stage, but in training the circle of light is widened to include the entire classroom.

Sharing the spotlight is perhaps the most important concept we can emphasize about your role as a workshop leader or trainer. Effective workshop leaders facilitate learning rather than simply lecturing at the participants. Because adult learning theory suggests that adults learn better when they are able to bring their own experiences to the classroom, a good facilitator will provide case studies, simulations, role-playing exercises, and other activities for the workshop interspersed

---

WOMEN IN THE TRAINING PROFESSION

As we discussed in Chapter One, women often prefer a more interactive public speaking style. Women may, in fact, gravitate toward careers as trainers because their style is so well suited to the profession. *Training and Development* magazine found that its female readership increased by 51 percent between 1983 and 1998, while the number of male subscribers decreased by 29 percent in this same period .

(Source: Shari Caudron. (1999, May). The Female Profession. *Training and Development*, 54.)

with brief lectures to deliver information. Such a format allows participants to draw their own conclusions through structured discussion about real-life application of the activities. Part of the fun in a workshop is the discovery aspect, or the "aha" experience, when participants see the application of the concept in their own lives.

Just as a speaker uses a variety of support materials (such as stories, statistics, and examples) to keep the speech interesting, a facilitator must incorporate a variety of methods to keep the training interesting, and appeal to a variety of learning styles. Some participants will learn best from role-playing exercises, while others will learn from videotapes, and still others from class discussion. Even in a two- or three-hour session, you can incorporate two or three types of activities to appeal to a variety of learning styles.

Naturally, we think a good trainer is one who is flexible and adept at on-the-spot audience analysis. This means you should be able to read your audience signals. Are they restless and in need of a break or energizing activity? Are they really enthusiastic about a topic and need more time? Are there a lot of confused looking faces out there? Participants will most certainly appreciate a facilitator who spots these signals and adds impromptu breaks, allows more discussion time when appropriate, or approaches a confusing topic in a new way. Similarly, it is absolutely the facilitator's job to rescue conversation from a monopolizing participant ("Thank you for sharing that idea; let's hear what some others think."); to redirect conversation that has gone off on a tangent ("These are interesting ideas, but let's get back now to our original goal of . . ."); and to redirect stalled discussion ("Let's look at a different aspect of this topic after a quick break."). Reading the nonverbal cues of the participants and acting accordingly is the most important skill a trainer can have.

One way to begin building a positive communication environment is by arriving early and making some quick adjustments to the training facility. Making the training room a welcoming place is a first step in setting up interaction while simultaneously enhancing your own credibility. Professor Bodenheimer always puts a simple welcome sign in the front of the room where she is training, has workbooks and other supplies set at each place before the participants arrive, and whenever possible has coffee or other refreshments available. This makes a good impression as soon as a participant walks in the door. Similarly, we recommend having all of your materials ready to go before the audience members start arriving. Then, as they begin to enter, you can walk around the room greeting individuals and introducing yourself; thus, you will already have a few friends in the audience when you begin.

Training itself is a huge industry and there are many, many volumes written about this type of public speaking. One way to get involved in a professional network of trainers is to become a member of your local chapter of the American Society of Training and Development. Consult the yellow pages or access the internet (http://www.astd.com) for more information about this organization. We also give you a few resources for further exploration in the box below.

SELECTED RESOURCES FOR TRAINING

Robert L. Craig. (Ed.). (1996). *The ASTD Training and Development Handbook: A Guide to Human Resource Development* (4th ed). New York: McGraw-Hill.

Andy Kirby. (1995). *Great Games for Trainers*. Amherst, MA: HRD Press.

Robert F. Mager. (1997). *Preparing Instructional Objectives* (3rd ed). Atlanta: Center for Effective Performance.

John W. Newstrom, Edward E. Scannell, and Carolyn D. Nilson. (1998). *The Complete Games Trainers Play, Volume II*. New York: McGraw-Hill.

Mel Silberman (Ed.). (2002). *The 2002 Training & Performance Sourcebook*. New York: McGraw-Hill.

Edie West. (1999). *The Big Book of Icebreakers: Quick, Fun Activities for Energizing Meetings and Workshops*. New York: McGraw-Hill.

CHAPTER SIX

Woman as Public Persona

The previous chapters in this book focus on technical issues of public speaking with attention to the many ways in which gender is a part of the speaking experience. After you have spent some time speaking in public, you will come to know yourself well. Why? Because speaking is one of the most personal forms of expression, in that it is a public display of identity connected to values, ideas, and attitudes. Language and nonverbal expression of self, which are the two major components of oral speech, express the most intimate nuance of you, the person. If your experience is similar to ours, then you will probably agree that getting up to speak in front of an audience is at once exhilarating and frightening—and, for women, a daunting moment of objectification. We have found that, often, we are the object of the audience's gaze purely because we are women. Given these public conditions, how do you express a persona that is comfortable and authentic? This is the key question that will be explored in this last chapter.

The American Heritage Dictionary defines *persona* as "the role that one assumes or displays in public or society; one's public image or personality, as distinguished from the inner self" ("Definition," 1992, p. 1351). In Latin, *persona* means mask, role, or person, and probably derives from the Etruscan *phersu* for mask. This chapter is about your identity as a public speaker, and the discussion invites you to think profoundly about what it is you choose to share with the public. Developing persona is about both masking and sharing, and we have many examples to go by as we lay out the groundwork for your decision making. Although this is the most theoretical chapter in the book, it is the one that may ultimately be most important to your long-term success as a public speaker. We invite you to return to this chapter often. Use it to help yourself mature as a speaker.

Obliteration and Objectification

Even a casual reading of the history of western civilization leads to one incontrovertible conclusion: women were never meant to take on the role of public speaker. Historical records are replete with stories, quotations, and admonitions for women to be silent (Ritchie & Ronald, 2001). Naturally, this led to the oxymoronic problem of the obliteration and objectification of woman as public speaker. This problem has not gone away, which is why we are writing a handbook for women speakers. Let's take time to investigate the historical context that surrounds you as a public speaker in a new century. Not only is such an investigation instructive, it places you in the position of having to strategize about your own persona and the ways in which you want to establish credibility for yourself and other women speakers.

As readers of rhetorical theory and persuasion history, we consistetly see three sources of hostility that have shaped a western view of women. They are the Bible, Aristotle, and Samuel Johnson. You may have read or heard these quotes in some form or fashion:

> Let the woman learn in silence with all subjection. But I suffer not a woman to teach, nor to usurp authority over the man, but to be in silence. (1 Timothy 2:11.12 KJV)

> The male is by nature fitter for command than the female. The courage of a man is shown in commanding, of a woman in obeying. The poet [Sophocles] says of women, "silence is a woman's glory." (Aristotle, 1943, pp. 267–269)

> Sir, a woman's preaching is like a dog's walking on his hind legs. It is not done so well, but you are surprised to find it done at all. (Johnson, 1929, p. 56)

Kathleen Hall Jamieson, dean of the Annenberg School of Communication at the University of Pennsylvania, has written extensively about women as speakers and leaders (we highly recommend her books). In a particularly incisive essay on the "effeminate" style, Jamieson begins with a description of the various ways men silenced women in colonial America: the ducking stool (near drowning as a tool to silence), the gag, and the gossip's bridle (bridling a woman like a horse to render the jaw immovable). She also describes how women who spoke in public were labeled as whores, hysterics, heresiarchs, witches, and shrills (Jamieson, 1988). And we wonder why women have a problem today.

The kind of history reported in the above discussion results in two ways of viewing women as public speakers: the first view is to obliterate women from the public platform, and the second view is to acknowledge women as public speakers but objectify them as sexually excessive or physically, spiritually, and mentally abnormal. Neither one of these views is acceptable, but we still see this kind of analysis applied to women today. For example, Patricia Ireland, former president of NOW, is often characterized as abnormal because she is lesbian and, therefore, not representative of most American women. Hillary Rodham Clinton was viewed by many voters as shrill and overly ambitious as first lady when she first moved into the White House. After her husband's confession regarding Monica Lewinsky, Mrs. Clinton was characterized in a national opinion poll as "strong, intelligent, brave, good, and loyal" ("First Lady," 1998, p. A5). Quite a turnaround, but one that matches perceptions of a first lady's "place."

Old, patriarchal ways of seeing the world are slow to change. Many people still believe that a woman's place is in the home, that women should occupy the private sphere in life while men occupy the public sphere. And, although we recognize a far different worldview, any woman who ascends the public platform must expect to grapple with the fact that some audience members will dismiss her outright just because she is a woman. Other audience members will gaze on her as a sexual being who can't be taken seriously or who is succeeding in spite of her biology. Some comments are simply tasteless, such as the description of the 1996 Republication National Convention keynote speaker. Witness Dan Rather's depiction of Congresswoman Susan Molinari as the "Republication Party's blond ambition" who one day could even be a vice presidential candidate. Savvy viewers of this television coverage surely did not miss the blond ambition reference as a possible Freudian slip relating Molinari to pop star Madonna.

Susan Molinari Switches Persona

Interestingly, after serving in the House of Representatives, Susan Molinari became a news broadcaster with CBS and a colleague of Dan Rather. Supporters hoped that her experience on the other side of the camera would contribute to her success in this new speaking role, but her first broadcast in September of 1997 was criticized in an almost tongue-and-cheek manner in a *New York Times* review by Abby Goodnough. Ms. Molinari was described as "chirping," "fidgeting," and living up to her "plucky image." Goodnough concluded that Ms. Molinari "seemed most comfortable discussing stomach exercises, movie stars and weather forecasts . . . [but] would take on weightier subjects as she gained experience" (p. 39). An in-depth essay in the *New York Times Magazine* in November of 1997 continued the exploration of her persona, leaving an overall negative impression about her confusing image and "tepid" ratings. In the summer of 1998, Molinari left CBS to devote time to her family.

(Sources: Elisabeth Bumiller. (1997, November 2). The Politics of Personality. *The New York Times Magazine*, 36–39. Abby Goodnough. (1997, September 14). Susan Molinari, Out of Congress and On Camera. *The New York Times* (national edition), 39. Susan Molinari. (1998.) *Representative Mom.* New York: Doubleday.)

One of the most disturbing attitudes we've encountered is the misogynist view that men need to silence women through sexual violence. In the fall of 1995, the following email message was circulated by male students at Cornell University. This message found its way onto computer screens across the country: "Top 75 reasons why women (bitches) should not have freedom of speech (Let's go back to the good old days when men were men and women were ribs) . . . #45. There are no speaking parts in pornos anyway . . . #38. Of course, if she can't speak, she can't say no . . . #20. This is my d—k. I'm gonna f—k you. No more stupid questions" (Cortina, Swan, Fitzgerald, & Waldo, 1998). If the men of Cornell found this funny, most women certainly did not. The outrageousness of the statement is so extreme that we have to wonder what kind of climate prevails not only on college campuses, but in American life in general. We want you to know that the mentality of women as dancing dogs is still with us and you should be aware that it cuts across class and racial lines.

However, all of this is not to say that you should approach your life as a speaker with fear or anger; rather, you should use your emotional response as motivation to tap into your intellectual capabilities and beat the patriarchal attitudes that still prevail. Developing a public persona will assist you in breaking down barriers and opening doors for yourself and other women. This approach of women helping women is eloquently discussed by journalist Cokie Roberts in her book entitled *We Are Our Mothers' Daughters* (1998). Her story about consumer advocate Esther Peterson is inspiration for all of us regarding the courage and strength it takes to become the voice for women. Against the prevailing attitudes of the 1950s, Peterson not only educated poor and working mothers, but spoke out for fair labor practices and safe food laws. Her tireless work resulted in a high-level appointment as an advocate for women's rights in the Kennedy administration.

Feminine Style on the Campaign Trail

Communication scholars Jane Blankenship and Deborah Robson (1995) studied countless speeches by women who serve in political positions across the country. They conclude that women's personal experiences help to shape a particular "feminine style" that is reflected in the public speaking of women running for public office or serving in governing positions. This feminine style is comprised of five characteristics:

1. Feminine political discourse bases political judgments on real experience. For example, women politicians who have been victims of domestic violence or who have been welfare mothers will advocate an agenda or participate in debate based on direct experience.
2. Feminine politicians value the inclusion of all types of people and consider the act of governing a public service rather than a career opportunity.

3. Feminine politicians see the power of public office as a way to "get things done" and to subsequently empower citizens to accomplish their goals.
4. Feminine politicians use a holistic approach to policy formation. In other words, a feminine style is not locked on one issue (for example, crime); rather, a host of interrelated issues are usually examined (for example, the antecedents of crime, crime itself, and the lives of criminals and their victims) as legislation is being formulated.
5. Feminine politicians are moving women's issues into the forefront of public awareness. Legislative agendas now have many more items related to domestic and family life than, say, twenty years ago.

Blankenship and Robson conclude that these five characteristics are tied to a shift in what Americans recognize as public versus private issues. As more women move into governing positions, the domestic, or private, sphere of life will shift more into the public eye. Depending upon your own reasons for engaging in public speaking, you may wish to consider how feminine style may actually be not only a component of the speech content, but a reflection of your persona. How might knowledge of the feminine characteristics assist you in presenting your values and attitudes to your public? The private-public dichotomy

---

WOMEN TO WATCH

In 1998, a nonpartisan public awareness campaign, called The White House Project, was launched with the idea of getting a woman into the White House. Twenty women were selected and put on a ballot so that the public could vote for their choices. Much interest has been generated by the Project, and names of previously unknown women are now becoming more familiar to the general public. A new initiative by The White House Project is called the Top of the Ticket Campaign. The goal is to put women on both the Democratic and Republican presidential tickets in 2004. If you are curious and would like to track this group of women, visit The White House Project website at http://www.thewhitehouseproject.org. You will see names such as Marian Wright Edelman, Kay Bailey Hutchison, Maxine Waters, Nancy Pelosi, and Christine Todd Whitman.

plays out in many ways, as we shall see in the following discussions about America's most visible women.

First Ladies

Margaret Truman, daughter of Bess and Harry Truman, has written a colorful and highly readable book entitled *First Ladies* (1995). In it, she weaves together the stories of all the first ladies as a study in public identity. We were struck by the message in Truman's book as it relates to the dramatic way the role of the first lady has changed in just the last forty years. In a similar vein, a *CBS Sunday Morning* segment featured stories about Mamie Eisenhower and Hillary Rodham Clinton that are worth comparing. Take a look at the quotes appearing in the box below. Mamie Eisenhower, in true 1950s style, fulfilled a public role by developing the persona of wife and supporter, but as we can see in Clinton's quote (and Truman's book depicts this as well), the 1990s paradigm was to chart a more vocal course of action. The step to public persona (as opposed to private person) is not without penalty. Early in her book, Truman discusses examples of America's criticism of recent first ladies, including Hillary Rodham Clinton, Roslyn Carter, and even Jacqueline Kennedy. Harsh criticism of seemingly insignificant (and sometimes private) matters, concluded Truman, "... raises the intriguing question of how much a First Lady can be herself—pursuing and enjoying what comes naturally to her—and remain this public person, who has suddenly become a symbol of American womanhood in all its myriad guises. It is a dilemma which every modern First Lady has to face" (p.10).

> "I never spoke out, but I was by Ike's side."
> Mamie Eisenhower
> Film Footage
>
> "As First Lady I don't have a formal role, but I intend to speak out."
> Hillary Rodham Clinton
> Interview with Martha Teischner
>
> (Source: *CBS Sunday Morning*, January 19, 1997.)

Although most of you do not look forward to becoming first lady, the point is that many of you will be female firsts: first CEO of your company, first mayor of your city, first chair of your school board, first president of the local Jaycee chapter, first representative to the state legislature. You are the women who will make things happen in your communities, and you are symbols of womanhood. How you choose to enact your symbolic status is part of your public persona. The fact that you are a woman adds a layer of complexity to the presentation of self on the public platform.

An instructive case study about how the complex identity of women can lead to distorted media representation can be seen in Ellen Reid Gold and Renee Speicher's analysis of Marilyn Quayle, an attorney by training and the spouse of former Vice President Dan Quayle. The authors analyzed newspaper coverage of Quayle over a twenty-nine-month period and found several common themes in the coverage: emphasis on clothing and hair with critical assessment of her choices, comparison of Quayle's intelligence to her husband's as a way to denigrate his competence as vice president, and criticism of Quayle's self-proclaimed role as adviser to her husband. Clearly, the press did not know how to handle Marilyn Quayle's interest in the public sphere, since most political wives, including former First Lady Barbara Bush, choose not to participate in their husbands' politics. Gold and Speicher describe Quayle's dilemma: "Intelligent and articulate, Marilyn Quayle struggled to establish a public persona which would enable her to claim those characteristics she valued: intelligence, competence, and the status associated with being a primary political adviser to her husband" (1995, p. 94). It wasn't until after Quayle apologized to the press in 1990 that criticism eased up somewhat. The case of Marilyn Quayle foreshadowed the experience of Hillary Rodham Clinton. Both of these women suffered greatly at the hands of the press for violating role expectations (centered on the idea of the obedient, doting wife) as they attempted to carve out public personas that reflected their true personalities and talents.

Someone who has escaped much of the brouhaha over who she is in public is Elizabeth Dole. It is fascinating to compare notes on Elizabeth Dole and Hillary Clinton, as the press did to the point of overkill during the 1996 presidential campaign. In July 1996, *Time* magazine ran a cover story entitled "Hillary vs. Liddy: Who Would Be the Better First Lady?" Interestingly, the content focused on Elizabeth

Dole rather than truly comparing the qualifications of the two women, even though both were noted as Methodists, daughters of prosperous fathers, and Ivy League lawyers (Gibbs & Duffy, 1996). The press conveyed that each woman was intensely private and held a certain amount of disdain for the reporters who often lurked nearby. Our more experienced readers will agree that no one ever gets used to having a camera in her face or a microphone shoved in front of her to get the latest comment. Just maintaining dignity is enough in such situations, and both Hillary Clinton and Elizabeth Dole have had plenty of experience practicing composure.

We argued in the beginning of this chapter that creating a persona is largely about making choices regarding what to share and what not to share with the public. Think about this description of Elizabeth Dole's persona: "Elizabeth Dole's life is always on message. Her syrupy charm and perfect manners do exactly what charm and manners are meant to do: persuade people to like her but not let them get too close. Her persona artfully conceals what she prefers to be hidden, namely that she is an opportunistic political infighter who has skillfully maneuvered every job she's ever had." A Dole staffer continues, "The public perception of her is the Southern belle. She can be that, but at heart she is a tough, no-nonsense, focused Washington bureaucrat" (Stengel, 1996, p. 32). Dole balances a public image based on her North Carolina roots with a private desire for a personal spirituality that often leaves the media wondering about the boundaries of this complex woman.

Hillary Clinton's complexity is no less than Elizabeth Dole's. A front page Sunday *New York Times* analysis of Hillary Clinton's role in the 1996 presidential campaign opened with the claim that she would head to the Democratic National Convention "by every available index the most controversial, unpopular First Lady in modern American history" (Purdum, 1996, p. 1). The analysis went on to argue that Hillary Clinton's step back from the public eye after the health care debacle clearly put the president back in control and eased the public's concern that she was vying for a copresidential role. Ironically, Hillary Clinton's interest in political policy set her up for a mixed reaction from the public. At the same time that she was viewed as overstepping her role as first lady, she was also viewed as a better choice for president than her own husband. Toward the end of the campaign, Elizabeth Dole was also seen as better qualified to be president.

Interestingly, both women found themselves in a double bind regarding the shaping of a public persona. Despite their qualifications, neither woman could appear to be too much of a political public servant, even though there are no official guidelines regarding the role and duties of the first lady. For Elizabeth Dole, the southern belle image worked well, while Hillary Clinton rearranged her priorities and stepped away from the glaring lights of Capitol Hill. As career women in the public eye, both have continued making choices about the public image each wishes to offer the American people. Hillary Clinton is more successful as a senator than she was as first lady, and Elizabeth Dole is now a senator from North Carolina.

The country's current first lady, Laura Bush, easily won public approval after her first six months in the White House, with 66 percent of the American people viewing her positively in a Pew Research Center poll ("Laura Bush," 2001). The poll reported that respondents described Mrs. Bush as "nice," "classy," "intelligent," "quiet", and "good." This is quite a contrast to Mrs. Clinton's first six months in the role, and approximates the more traditional notions of what Americans seem to want in a first lady. It is interesting to note that President George W. Bush surrounds himself with female aides who have a more masculine communication style than the first lady. His closest female counselors are Karen Hughes, speechwriter and first director of his communication offices, and Condoleezza Rice, National Security Advisor. Both are viewed by the press as highly influential in the Bush administration and much admired for their straightforward approach, sense of humor, and love of sports ("Bush's Top Female Aide," 2001; Reed, 2001; Sanger, Shanker, & Perlez, 2001).

Queens and Prime Ministers

America spends almost as much time watching female public figures in the United Kingdom as we do watching our first lady. Queen Elizabeth has largely escaped being the target of negative press, although the monarchy, as an institution, and her children have been the object of intense, often nasty, scrutiny. The queen rarely errs in her public appearances; she has had over forty years to develop a public persona suited to her role as queen of England. Her public speeches are planned down to the most minute detail, and she has reading glasses and note cards handy. She has the respect of her citizens on a personal level, and she executes her role with intelligence, diplomacy, and dignity. Queen Elizabeth is also known as a monarch with a sense of wit. Even in the aftermath of Princess Diana's death, the citizens appeared to be criticizing the monarchy as an out-of-date institution rather than Queen Elizabeth herself. Although it remains to be seen how much of an influence on Queen Elizabeth's persona the death of Diana will have, the press reported with some pleasure that the queen's Christmas message for 1997 "showed the lighter, more personal touch that has been in evidence since Diana's death, when the royal family was criticized for being remote and behind the times" (Lederer, 1997, p. A2). (We want to note that Princess Diana's persona largely reflected her interpersonal skills in one-on-one interactions rather than her persona as a public speaker. Because of this important distinction, we are not going to spend time analyzing Diana's persona.)

A more controversial example of British public persona is former Prime Minister Margaret Thatcher. As the first woman in the prime minister role, Mrs. Thatcher was a source of both admiration and perplexity for many of her constituents. Dubbed the Iron Lady (not the Iron Maiden, as the American press erroneously reported it) by the Soviets, she displayed a public image that consisted of a lacquered personal style—coiffed hair, two-piece suits, the signature scarab bracelet—and a measured, quick-witted style of public speaking that showed evidence of thorough preparation and immeasurable confidence (confidence that was often interpreted as arrogance). Mrs. Thatcher's public persona may not have been too far from her personal identity, but Queen Elizabeth is a more complex combination of personal and public identity. Her longevity in global public life is a fascinating example of how one lives a public role while maintaining a sense of balance with private identity. Mrs. Thatcher, Queen Elizabeth, and the American first ladies are examples of how much sacrifice one makes to serve a public constituency.

WORLD LEADERS

To learn more about both the personas and the politics of fifteen of the world's women leaders, read Laura Liswood's biographies, which are based on first-person interviews and compiled in her book *Women World Leaders: Fifteen Great Politicians Tell Their Stories* (published by New York University Press in 1996). You will enjoy finding out about a diverse group of women, including Corazon Aquino of the Philippines and Mary Robinson of Ireland.

Women of Color

Much of this chapter, so far, has concentrated on the lives of Caucasian women. We recognize that modern life involves the participation of all women and that there may be some different considerations for women of color when it comes to developing persona in a "white" world covered by a "white" press. Much of the theorizing about African American women, and by implication women of other races, is that women of color who communicate publicly face a double jeopardy: being a woman and being a person of color. As public speakers, we think our readers should understand the situation of double jeopardy a little more clearly before stepping out on the public platform, although we recognize that persons of color experience these situations and learn coping strategies at very early ages. We believe that it is important to share our observations and analyses of women of color as a way to learn from each other and promote success for all women on the public platform.

We have already seen above how two women like Hillary Rodham Clinton and Elizabeth Dole can share many similarities, but evoke different responses from audiences. Another pair of women who appear to affect the American public in the same bifurcated way are Joycelyn Elders and Shirley Chisholm. Both Elders and Chisholm are African American public servants and political figures in mainstream America. Chisholm, educated as a teacher, was the first African American woman elected to Congress and was a Democratic nominee for president in 1972. Elders, trained as a physician specializing in pediatric endocrinology, served as the state health director of Arkansas under Governor Bill Clinton. She then became surgeon general of the United States under President Clinton. Both Elders and Chisholm have worked all their lives to empower women, but Chisholm will go down in history as a great civil rights leader and advocate for the Equal Rights Amendment, while Elders will be remembered as the radical doctor who advocated for legalization of drugs and free condoms for America's teenagers.

How could Dr. Elders project a persona so misunderstood that she eventually left the office of the surgeon general under pressure? The following excerpt from a 1994 interview, conducted by Claudia Dreifus of the *New York Times Magazine,* gives us some insight:

> Q: U.S. News and World Report described you this way: 'She's intolerant, preachy, judgmental and overbearing. She's bright, articulate, passionate and kind.' Is that an accurate description?
> A: It's . . . pretty good. I'm only overbearing to the people I need to be overbearing with. You've got to get people's attention before you can achieve change. As Surgeon General, you have to take a stand. People are either going to love you or hate you. (p. 19)

Surgeon General Elders was on a mission to give women, especially poor women, reproductive freedom of choice. Given her agenda, she spared no criticism of government officials and parents as the people responsible for teenage pregnancy and all its implications in this country. Talking about taboo topics like sex, reproductive responsibility, and pregnancy prevention did not go over well with many conservative lawmakers and voters. More insulting to Dr. Elders, as she conveyed in the *New York Times Magazine* interview, was the overt racism and sexism expressed toward her during her confirmation hearing and from a segment of the American Medical Association who did not apparently know that Elders was a physician. What damaged Dr. Elders' public image the most, however, was the impression that she herself was an irresponsible parent because her own twenty-eight-year-old son was arrested on drug charges. Never mind that her son was an adult and responsible for his own conduct; the public pressured the surgeon general out of office. Moral of the story: when people do not like what you have to say or how you look, they will find ways to promote you and your message as a negative entity, regardless of your qualifications or the logic of your stance on the issues. Moreover, if you are a woman of color, there are often racist and sexist motivations at work to prevent you from reaching the public platform in the first place, or to derail you if you manage to arrive. This is what we meant earlier when talking about double jeopardy.

In contrast, Shirley Chisholm, now in her seventies, has achieved something of star status in this country. Professor Natalle saw Chisholm speak at a Martin Luther King, Jr. celebration in 1997 at UNCG, where she was introduced as the "greatest civil rights worker and African American woman—a living legend who will go down in history with Harriett Tubman." Chisholm's celebratory speech about Dr. King's vision emulated the characteristics of Afrocentric discourse described by communication professor Adetokunbo F. Knowles-Borishade (1994). Chisholm served as the caller who invoked the word to responders to create spiritual harmony. The stage was set by a spiritual that was sung just before she rose to speak. She then called the audience to direct action to combat racism and poverty in America, and she argued that we should rise up, based on our sense of moral responsibility and concern for social justice. Her speaking style consisted of excellent pacing in a preacher cadence with emphasis on appropriate words, emotional conviction, strong imagery ("the federal government is a tail light rather than a headlight for economic justice"), and the linkage of God to "our struggle for justice." As Chisholm exhorted her audience to direct action by invoking Martin Luther King Jr.'s dream for freedom, the audience responded with applause. There was an electric connection between Chisholm and her largely student audience, and they rewarded her afterward with gifts and requests for autographs. She seemed to enjoy every minute of the evening and relished her role as a model for political inspiration.

Today, much of Chisholm's speaking schedule revolves around Black History Month and Women's History Month, and she is selectively seen in celebratory situations where her persona is one of living legend. Chisholm continues to live up to the expectations of her audiences. In retirement, she can finish shaping her persona as she wishes to be remembered. Joycelyn Elders, however, has not fared so well with either the "white" power structure or the African American community. Now that Elders is on the college speaking circuit, perhaps she can soften her image.

On a different note, National Security Advisor Condoleezza Rice is not a person to waste time on pleasing an audience based on their expectations. In her speech to the Republication National Convention (2000), she delivered a memorized and serious pep talk in which she repeated, "I found a party that treats me like an individual." Her claim that "freedom depends on our strength of force" is an apt reflection of Condoleezza Rice as a person; her expertise is in Russian history and military policy. She is a show of force in style and speech and, unlike many African American public figures who serve the Democratic Party, she represents the individualism of Republican politics. This is a different kind of persona for American audiences, and it will be interesting to see if she sets new criteria for success on the public platform.

Negotiating Persona With Your Public

In writing this chapter on public persona, we have come to realize that you do not make choices in isolation about what to share and what to mask as your persona develops. Two factors influence your choices and put you in the position of having to negotiate the image you want. First, there are expectations from the public itself about who or what you should be, and those expectations are grounded in old-fashioned norms about sex, race, and class. Second, the media makes choices for you by the way it reports on you or what the story says about you. It would be wise to think about these factors as you step out on the public platform, so let's spend a little time talking about each one.

A theme that emerges from the discussions about first ladies and women of color is that the public often already has ideas about how you should play a role and the kind of image you should project. When you don't conform to expectations, people get confused. Clearly, this is a problem for women who are in ill-defined roles such as first lady (Anderson, forthcoming). But the same can be said for other roles that are not so poorly defined. When Patty Murray ran for senator in the state of Washington, she was dubbed "a mom in tennis shoes." That mom in tennis shoes is now in Washington, D.C. doing what she can to make life better for her constituents back home, just like any senator would do. The first female mayor of Greensboro, North Carolina, was dubbed "a tree hugger," but that tree hugger served three terms in office and advocated just as hard for economic growth as she did for environmental control, just like any good mayor would do. Women stepping out to perform public service must be prepared for some confusion on the public's part, especially if the public is not used to the idea that a woman might be qualified for the job. The tree hugger and the mom in tennis shoes retained a sense of humor (epithets like those tend to stick), but they also negotiated identities that included credible performances and intelligent decision making.

Women of color often face several sets of expectations, some from the "white" community and some from their own ethnic or racial community. In reading the book *Diversity in Public Communication* (Kelly, Laffoon, & McKerrow, 1994), it became clear to us that members of the Chicano, African American, and Native American communities probably expect representatives of their communities to exhibit a particular public speaking style. In other words, the public expects the speaker to be a reflection of the cultural traditions that characterize that particular racial or ethnic community. If a speaker does not live up to expectations, nonconformance will lead to penalty. This was made clear in a *New York Times Magazine* article by Kristal Brent Zook in which she argued for a plurality of representation regarding African American women's identity. The photographs accompanying the text showed three groups of women leaders: "The Three Queens" (Coretta Scott King, Myrlie Evers-Williams, and Betty Shabazz [widows of slain civil rights leaders]), "The Progressive Bridge" (Angela Davis, Jewell Jackson McCabe, and Kimberle Crenshaw [academic social activists]), and "The New Guard" (the author, Kimberly Weaver, and Rebecca Walker [young intellectuals interested in crossing race and sex barriers]). This page of photographs goes beyond the double jeopardy consciousness we expressed earlier in this chapter to bring up issues about persona and age, sexual orientation, experience, and a host of other factors that comprise a person's makeup. No one else is a Coretta

Scott King, but often the public forgets that and projects a series of expectations onto a speaker that simply cannot be met.

Speaking of expectations, Professor Natalle witnessed an interesting situation regarding the public presentation of self for African American and Caucasian women. At a Women's Equality Day celebration in 1996, which occurred simultaneously with a North Carolina Equity agenda setting workshop at Bennett College (an all-female, African American college in Greensboro, North Carolina), there were about an equal number of African American and Caucasian participants. It was a hot, humid day in August, and the air conditioning was malfunctioning in the building where we met. The dress code for the African American participants was clearly dress-up and business attire—beautiful floral prints, silk, African prints, high heels, and pantyhose. The Caucasian women, however, arrived in casual wear such as sleeveless blouses, flowing skirts (which included the attire of the keynote speaker), sandals, and shorts. There was a significant difference in how the two groups presented themselves. Later, as people were complaining about the air conditioning problem, I discovered that this building had the same problem every year, yet the representatives from Bennett College attempted to look professional (ignoring their own personal comfort) even under such wilting conditions. As President Gloria Scott stood on the platform to welcome the audience, I marveled at her ability to look gorgeous and set an example for her faculty, staff, and students while simultaneously projecting an image to other citizens of Greensboro that the women of Bennett are professionals under any circumstances. Clearly, there were two very different sets of self-imposed expectations among the participants in this activity that demarcated a set of norms related to the racial backgrounds of the women. At a Sigma Gamma Rho forum, which was held at UNCG in November 2002, the speakers confirmed that African American women dress professionally as a criterion of public credibility (Sigma Gamma Rho, 2002).

The Media Factor

What about the media factor? In this chapter we frequently mention the media as a powerful force that sometimes makes choices for

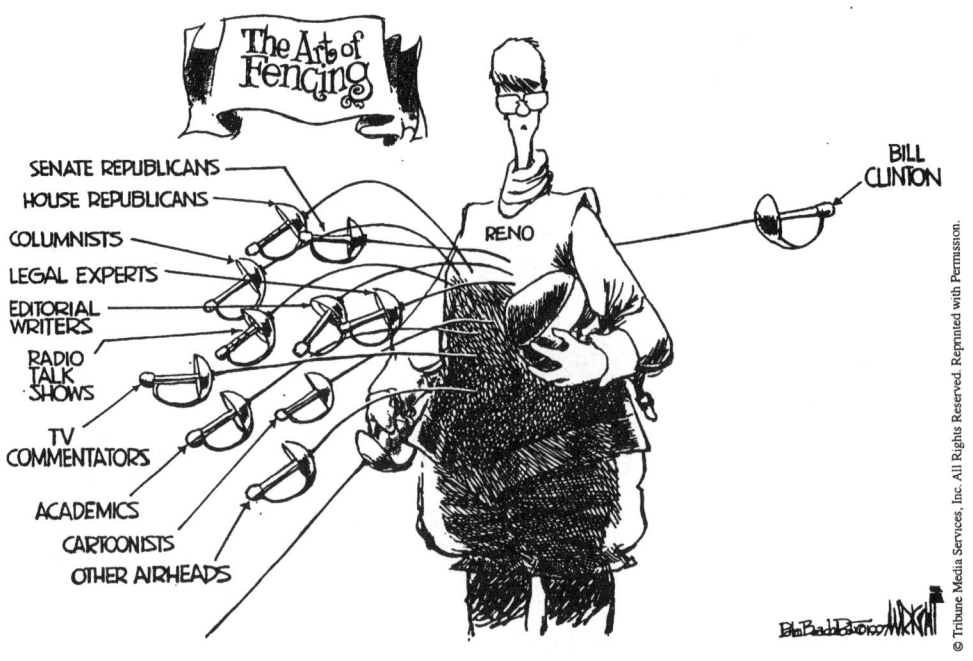

you. We want to emphasize that we are not against the media; rather, we recognize the pervasiveness of the media in our lives. If you choose to be visible on the public platform, your persona will be shaped by you and the media. We suggest that you think carefully about whether or not you may need a media consultant, someone who will not only help you with delivery skills, but someone who will help you decide about content and information sharing. Even the most experienced women are frustrated by the media's (mis)interpretation of the persona they would like to project.

Former Attorney General Janet Reno is one person who received constant criticism from the press, and we suspect that part of this criticism was the result of a press who just did not understand Reno's style. A Sunday edition of the *New York Times* featured Reno on the front page with the headline "Reno's Loner Image Belies a More Complex Reality" (Johnston & Sontag, 1997). In this interesting analysis, the writers talked about the frequent mismatch between Reno's persona and her performance as attorney general. She was described as "plainspoken," "inscrutable," "driven," and "possessing remarkable personal integrity," while her public speech was described as "wooden, guarded and platitudinous" (p. 1). Such juxtapositions of public and private clearly set up confusion and misunderstanding. To make matters worse, an entire analysis of Reno based on her height and size was presented in the *Washington Post Magazine* (Mundy, 1998). What could be more irrelevant to her professional expertise? Yet, the story fueled the controversy. Reno herself told CBS interviewer Rita Braver, "You get used to being damned. It's important that people laugh at themselves" (Reno, 1999). The editorial cartoon lampooning Reno speaks for itself.

Anita Hill, who testified against Clarence Thomas in his U.S. Supreme Court nomination hearing, may be the most extreme example

---

THE ULTIMATE DILEMMA:
A MEDIA EXPERT WHO IS MISUNDERSTOOD BY THE MEDIA

Kathleen Hall Jamieson revealed in a speech (1996a), and later in a conversation with Professor Natalle (1996b), that she was vexed by the media's inability to recognize that she wishes to be seen as a "public intellectual" rather than a "political pundit." Because Jamieson uses irony as a way to analyze political speech, she is viewed as someone who is making witty commentary on the political scene. Just the contrary. Jamieson, the dean of the Annenberg School of Communication, is the head of a research program that systematically catalogues arguments, political platforms, public opinion, and media coverage of most of the political process going on in the country. If you listen to Dean Jamieson give a speech, her repertoire of statistical knowledge quickly lets you know that she is a serious analyst of politics. The problem with America, says Jamieson, is that we don't have a category for the public intellectual. The only thing the media knows about is the political pundit, hence the error. To Jamieson, and her academic colleagues, the error is serious because she is often left out of the political dialogue (controlled by her media colleagues) where her point of view would not only be useful, but necessary for a complete understanding of the political communication process in this country. If she is invited to the dialogue, it is often for entertainment purposes rather than serious contribution. Should Dr. Jamieson adjust her strategy, or should she find ways to better educate media professionals about how she wishes to be portrayed?

in recent times of someone who has been thoroughly "raked over the coals" and presented almost in caricature. You may also wish to consider Kathleen Hall Jamieson's predicament as further food for thought on this topic.

One public figure who did a good job working with the media to achieve her agenda is Madeleine Albright. In an analysis of her first six months as secretary of state, *Washington Post* staff writer Michael Dobbs (1997) touched on all the positive strategies used by Albright, including a clear understanding of her audiences. She connected with both the American public and members of Congress (remember images of her walking arm-in-arm with Jesse Helms?) in order to put foreign policy high on the national agenda. In the male-dominated world of power politics, Albright found a way to combine machismo and femininity to appeal to everyone; in other words, she found a way to meet the double standards society has set up for women on the public platform. As one consultant told Dobbs, "Albright is one of the few top female politicians who has succeeded in projecting an image of strength without being called a bitch" (p. A11). Another public figure who is well liked by the media is Bennett College president Johnnetta Cole. Considered a "superstar," Cole is the former president of Spelman College who knows how to jumpstart African American women's colleges (Johnson, 2002). The press likes her style. She is genuine, warm, spiritual, and humorous. Cole uses the press to advance her educational agenda, and the press covers events where Cole is speaking.

Prepare A Media Kit

Even if you do not need to hire a media consultant, we offer a practical suggestion: prepare a media kit as a first step in shaping your public persona. The kit should include a fact sheet, or bio, about yourself and your accomplishments. Prepare a short press release that offers a narrative version of your biographical sketch. Include a recent photograph of yourself so that you have one ready if you need to furnish a photo to the media. Engaging in this exercise will force you to make choices about what you want to share with your public. To learn more about media kits, consult a standard text in public relations such as

Newsom and Carrell's *Public Relations Writing*. Take a look at the box below for a synopsis of what a media kit should contain. In this age of high technology, you might want to think about adding a CD-ROM or DVD as part of the contents of your media kit. If you decide to go this route, label all your disks clearly with a title. If you plan to run for public office, another good source of information about preparing media kits is the 1995 National Women's Political Caucus guidebook called *Campaigning to Win*, which we have listed in the references for this chapter. Don't forget: there are university communication professors who might help you in addition to professional PR practitioners. And remember that you need not spend a lot of money to accomplish the purpose of a media kit, which is to provide valuable information to the media.

CONTENTS OF A MEDIA KIT

Doug Newsom and Bob Carrell give the following tips for assembling a media kit:

1. Make sure the kit contains publicity material that an editor can easily access and use. The information should be correct, up to date, and targeted to specific media (for example, print, television, radio).
2. The kit should contain a one-page news release about your accomplishments, a bio, a fact sheet, and eight-by-ten-inch black-and-white glossy photographs that reproduce clearly.
3. Package the materials in an attractive, but functional, folder or binder that is labeled on the front with your name.

(Source: Doug Newsome & Bob Carrell. (2001). *Public Relations Writing: Form and Style.* Belmont, CA: Wadsworth Publishers, pp. 348–350.)

Gender Identity Politics

Finally, a word on gender identity politics. This is a phrase that readers may not be familiar with because it is a relatively new concept. There are some individuals and groups who participate in social and political change processes by specifically drawing attention to gendered issues and themselves as gendered beings. For example, the AIDS Coalition to Unleash Power (ACT UP) is an organization dedicated to drawing attention in dramatic fashion to the AIDS crisis. Most of the speakers in ACT UP are gay men who make the argument that attitudes toward gay men and AIDS, as a gay issue, hinder the progress toward finding a medical cure for AIDS. Gay identity is intricately bound up with the people and the issue as it is presented to the public, and gender identity is explicit in the political agenda.

When we think about gender identity and political process as women, it takes us back to one of the original slogans of the women's movement in the 1960s: "The personal is political." The idea is that women's experiences are so tightly bound to the political life of the culture that changes in their personal lives are political acts. In rhetorical theory, there is a belief that once someone other than a Caucasian heterosexual man gets up on the public platform to argue an issue, we suddenly have gendered politics, hence gendered argument. Professor Catherine Helen Palczewski claims that "gender always influences all aspects of argument—form, function, reception, and presentation" (p. 162). What Palczewski means is that if you are a feminist (or a womanist, or a lesbian, or a heterosexual homemaker), then your gender identity may very well influence who you are, how you argue your issue, and how audiences will respond to you. We think this is a reasonable and highly probable interpretation of how life is in the public arena. If you shape a public persona based in feminism, then there are deep implications for all aspects of your life in the community.

We encourage you to think about gender identity politics because the phrase is showing up more frequently. In fact, you may wish to consult a special issue of the *New York Times Magazine* published in November of 1996 and entitled "Heroine Worship: Inventing an Identity in the Age of Female Icons." Over thirty women, from Audrey Hepburn to Marian Anderson, are featured in short essays describing their iconic characteristics. In the introduction to the essays, Holly Brubach writes, "In the spirit of post-modernism, we piece ourselves together, assembling the examples of several women in a single personality—a process that makes for some unprecedented combinations, like Madonna: the siren who lifts weights and becomes a mother" (p. 57). Before you chuckle, think about Patty Murray, the mom in tennis shoes and United States senator, who ran on a platform to attack the national deficit, put people back to work, and deal with problems that directly concern the family. Politics and gender identity are intertwined and they do influence the public persona of the speaker.

Breakpoint! After reading this chapter, respond to the following questions:

What do you want your public persona to be?

What are you willing to share with your public?

How much of your life do you wish to keep private?

Do you need a media consultant?

What strategies will you use to create a public persona?

Epilogue

Self-Diagnosis and Action Plan

You may now breathe a sigh of relief. You've read all the chapters in this handbook and now realize that you already have some skills as a public speaker. You also realize that there are areas that need improvement. Finally, you've probably noticed that our point of view favors some key ideas about the relationship of women to public speaking. We have encouraged you to think about your public speaking as a series of choices that will help you develop into not only the best technical speaker, but the best person you are capable of being. We have noted that many of your choices are rooted in a world that pays close attention to sex differences, gender, and the values we place on the public expression of ourselves as gendered beings. You have much to think about and many decisions to make. Where to begin? Do you need to reassess the diagnosis of strengths and weaknesses that you did at the end of the introduction? Now is the time to do so.

Speaking Diagnosis

Strengths as a speaker:

_____

_____

_____

_____

Weaknesses as a speaker:

_____

_____

_____

_____

Next, we want you to write down an action plan that you will commit to following over the next several months. Your plan should be a result of your diagnosis above. Review this action plan every month until you've reached your goals.

ACTION PLAN

Goal #1:

_____

_____

Strategy to Reach Goal:

_____

_____

Goal #2:

_____

_____

Strategy to Reach Goal:

_____

_____

Goal #3:

_____

_____

Strategy to Reach Goal:

_____

_____

Take advantage of the pullout tools at the end of the handbook as practical components of your strategies to reach your goals. Finally, we leave you with our rules for success. Good luck! We enjoyed sharing what we know with you and hope that you will send your public speaking experiences to us. Women helping women is what this handbook is all about.

The Woman Speaker's Ten Rules for Success—Two Versions

Jody's Rules

1. Be yourself. Develop skills that enhance your personal style.
2. Never forget that you are in public. Diplomacy is your best ally.
3. Base your public speaking on ethics. An ethical speaker will never go wrong.
4. Retain your sense of humor. It is your defense against insanity.
5. Be prepared. Not even experienced speakers can last long without preparation.
6. Know yourself. Your strengths highlight your abilities; your weaknesses promote humility.
7. Speak from your experience. Life is what guides us to wisdom.
8. Listen to your audience. Effective communication is both speaking and listening.
9. Keep a journal. Recording your experiences shows you patterns of success and weakness.
10. Learn to use a microphone. It's the biggest technical problem speakers have to overcome.

Postnote: At a dinner party, a savvy attorney, who had just argued a case before the North Carolina Supreme Court, asked me what makes a good speaker. The teacher in me wanted to run down my list above, but I was so engaged in our conversation about women as speakers—we had been discussing the platform personas of Ruth Bader Ginsberg, Madeleine Albright, and Hillary Rodham Clinton—that I just spoke from my heart. I said that a truly good speaker has three things going for her. First, she is experienced, so that worrying about technical details or saying "um" in the wrong place just won't happen. In other words, she is smooth and has her technique down pat. Second, she has a level of charisma that will draw the audience to her. And, finally, she has something important to say that the audience wants to hear.

In looking back over the ten rules, these three characteristics are easily tied in. This handbook will teach you some things about technique, and we certainly advocate that you have something important to say. But the charisma—which involves a whole host of things like confidence, charm, eloquence, and the ability to create rapport—you will have to develop on your own. Charisma is inside you as part of your public persona, so we hope you will find in yourself what appeals to others and use that to your best advantage.

Fritzi's Rules

1. Know your topic, know your topic, know your topic.
2. Develop an outline and talk (not read) through it ten to fifteen times in rehearsal.
3. Stand up straight.
4. Start your preparation early so you can skip the apologies.
5. Arrive at least forty-five minutes in advance.
6. Plan a rehearsal session with your visual aids.
7. Incorporate real-life examples and stories wherever possible.
8. Articulate—let the audience hear every sound.
9. Smile.
10. Reward yourself—chocolate or otherwise.

Postnote: Shortly after the terrorist attacks on September 11, 2001, a woman called into a radio talk show complaining about the lack of women's voices in the debate over how the United States should respond. The caller was right. According to a 1998 Freedom Forum report entitled *Who Speaks for America? Sex, Age and Race on the Network News*, 87 percent of expert sound bites are provided by men. And if you read your local newspaper, many of the opinion columns are likely to be written by men. What this means is that women's voices are being left out of important conversations about our neighborhoods and our nation. Free speech is a critical component of democracy. When the stock market falls, unemployment rises, or terrorists attack, we don't take to the streets looting and rioting. In our country, we discuss and debate. Public speaking can give women a voice in these important deliberations.

Finding your voice may have some added benefits as well. A few years ago, after delivering a one-minute presentation to a professional networking group, Women of Washington, a striking and poised woman approached me and said, "I enjoyed your presentation and would love to get to know you." Today that woman is one of my best friends. If a one-minute speech can offer as great a reward as a lifelong friend, we must let our voices be heard!

Bibliography

Introduction

Albright Adds Substance to Style. (1997, April 20). *Greensboro News & Record,* A11.

Center for American Women and Politics (CAWP). (n.d.). Women Who Will Serve in the 108th Congress 2003–05. http://www.cawp.rutgers.edu. [accessed January 22, 2003].

Faludi, Susan. (1992a, January 26). Speak for Yourself. *New York Times Magazine,* 10, 29.

Faludi, Susan. (1992b, October 25). C-SPAN's Author Interview. http://www.booknotes.org/transcript/?programID=1121. [accessed November 10, 2002].

Freedman, Dan. (1999, January 5). Red Cross Leader Steps Down to Consider "New Paths." *Greensboro News & Record,* A1, A4.

Garland, Jasper V. (1938). *Public Speaking for Women.* New York: Harper & Bros. Publishers.

House Welcomes Record Number of Minority Members. (2003, January 7*). Greensboro News & Record*, A3.

Jaasma, Marjorie A. (1997). Classroom Communication Apprehension: Does Being Male or Female Make a Difference? *Communication Reports, 10,* 219–228.

Nonkin, Lesley Jane. (1987, May). Fear of Speaking. *Vogue,* 161, 163.

Palczewski, Catherine Helen. (1996). Argumentation and Feminism: An Introduction. *Argumentation and Advocacy, 32,* 161–169.

Richardson, Eudora Ramsay. (1936). *The Woman Speaker: A Hand-Book and Study Course on Public Speaking.* Richmond, VA: Whittet & Shepperson, Publishers.

Steinem, Gloria. (1984). Speech to Webster College delivered March 1973. In Anita Taylor (Ed.), *Speaking in Public* (2nd ed.) (284–292). Englewood Cliffs, NJ: Prentice-Hall.

Steinem, Gloria. (1998, October 22). *The Politics of Sexuality*. Reynolds Lecture delivered to Davidson College, Davidson, NC.

The White House Project. (2001, December 5). *Who's Talking? An Analysis of Sunday Morning Talk Shows*. New York: Author.

Walter Scott's Personality Parade. (1997, May 11). *Parade Magazine*, 4.

Weisul, Kimberly. (2002, April 8). Does Giving a Speech Spook Women More? *Business Week*, 12.

Chapter One: Preparing the Message

Adubato, Steve. (1998). Speaking Styles of the Sexes. *Business News New Jersey, 11*, 19.

Crawford, Mary. (1995). *Talking Difference: On Gender and Language*. Thousand Oaks, CA: Sage Publications.

Daly, Mary. (1995, April 28). *Outrageous, Contagious Women*. Speech delivered at The University of North Carolina at Greensboro, Greensboro, NC.

Di Mare, Lesley. (1992). Rhetoric and Women: The Private and the Public Spheres. In L. A. M. Perry, L. H. Turner, & H. M. Sterk (Eds.), *Constructing and Reconstructing Gender: The Links Among Communication, Language, and Gender* (45–50). Albany: State University of New York Press.

Faludi, Susan. (1992, January 26). Speak for Yourself. *The New York Times Magazine*, 10, 29.

Farrell, T. J. (1979). The Female and Male Modes of Rhetoric. *College English, 40*, 909–921.

Foss, Karen A., & Foss, Sonja K. (1989). Incorporating the Feminist Perspective in Communication Scholarship: A Research Perspective. In K. Carter & C. Spitzack (Eds.), *Doing Research on Women's Communication: Perspectives on Theory and Method* (65–91). Norwood, NJ: Ablex.

Foss, Karen A., & Foss, Sonja K. (2003). *Inviting Transformation: Presentational Speaking for a Changing World*. Prospect Heights, IL: Waveland Press.

Foss, Sonja K., & Griffin, Cindy L. (1995). Beyond Persuasion: A Proposal for an Invitational Rhetoric. *Communication Monographs, 62*, 2–18.

Frobish, Todd S. (2000). Jamieson Meets Lucas: Eloquence and Pedagogical Model(s) in The Art of Public Speaking. *Communication Education, 49*, 239–252.

Jaffe, Clella. (2001). *Public Speaking: A Cultural Perspective* (3rd ed.). Belmont, CA: Wadsworth Publishing Company.

Jamieson, Kathleen Hall. (1988). *Eloquence in an Electronic Age: The Transformation of Political Speechmaking.* New York: Oxford University Press.

Stephenson, Karen. (1992, December 15). How to Lead People: An Anthropological Perspective on an MBA Education. *Vital Speeches of the Day,* 138–141.

Tannen, Deborah (1990). *You Just Don't Understand: Men and Women in Conversation.* New York: William Morrow.

Tannen, Deborah. (1994). *Talking 9 to 5.* New York: William Morrow.

Tweeten, Taresa. (1992). *An Evaluation of Form and Structure: The Speech Making of Elizabeth Cady Stanton and Martin Luther King, Jr.* Unpublished master's thesis, University of North Carolina at Greensboro.

Tweeten, Taresa. (1997, July). Personal correspondence with Professor Bodenheimer.

Chapter Two: Relating to the Audience

Barreca, Regina. (1991). *They Used to Call Me Snow White . . . But I Drifted: Women's Strategic Use of Humor.* New York: Penguin Books.

Barreca, Regina (Ed.). (1996). *The Penguin Book of Women's Humor.* New York: Penguin Books.

Blow, Richard. (1996). Outspoken: What Patricia Wants. *Mother Jones, 21,* 70–71.

Broder, John M. (1997, October 26) For the First Lady at 50, a New Start. *The New York Times* (national edition), 14.

Campbell, Karlyn Kohrs. (1989). *Man Cannot Speak for Her* (Vol. 1). Westport, CT: Greenwood Press.

Chisholm, Shirley. (1997, January 29). Keynote Speech at 11th Annual MLK, Jr. Celebration Program. University of North Carolina, Greensboro, NC.

Conner-Greene, Patricia. (1996). The Influence of Gender and Language on Evaluations of Speaker Characteristics and Perceived Persuasion. Unpublished manuscript, Department of Psychology, Clemson University.

Dole, Elizabeth. (1996, August 22). Speech delivered at Dole/Kemp Rally. Koury Convention Center, Greensboro, NC.

Dworkin, Andrea. (1985, January 12). Speech delivered at Duke University. Durham, NC.

Ferraro, Geraldine. (1982, November 15). Who Will Fight For the Worth of Women's Work? *Vital Speeches of the Day,* 70–73.

First Lady Drawing Admiration for Strength. (1998, August 29). *Greensboro News & Record,* A5.

Fisher, Mary. (1996, August 12). Speech delivered to the Republican National Convention. San Diego, CA. *CBS News.*

Gerhart, Ann. (2001, September 18). Laura Bush, Comforter in Chief. *The Washington Post.* http://www.washingtonpost.com/wp-dyn/articles/A52751-2001Sep18.html. [accessed September 19, 2001].

Goodman, Ellen. (1998, June 21). Politics and the Pregnant Mom. *Greensboro News & Record,* F4.

Hovland, Carl I., Janis, Irving L., & Kelley, Harold H. (1953). *Communication and Persuasion.* New Haven: Yale University Press.

Kilbourne, Jean. (1996, Fall). *Still Killing Us Softly.* Speech delivered at the University of North Carolina at Greensboro, Greensboro, NC.

Konner, Joan. (1990, September 15). Women in the Marketplace. *Vital Speeches of the Day,* 726–727.

McKinnon, Jackie. (1996, August 24). *Overview of Agenda Process.* Speech delivered at the 3rd Biennial Agenda Program with NC Equity, Bennett College, Greensboro, NC.

Natalle, Elizabeth J. (in press). Jacqueline Kennedy and the Rhetorical Construction of Camelot. In Molly M. Wertheimer (Ed.), *Inventing Their Voices: The Rhetoric of American First Ladies of the Twentieth Century.* New York: Rowman and Littlefield.

Pearce, Kimber Charles, & Natalle, Elizabeth J. (1993). Deconstructing Gender Differences in Persuasibility: A Bricolage. *Women's Studies in Communication, 16,* 55–73.

Poll Respondents Give Nod to Clintons as Most Admired. (1999, January 1). *Greensboro News & Record,* A5.

Reagan, Nancy. (1996, August 12). Speech delivered to the Republican National Convention. San Diego, CA. *CBS News.*

Report on Hillary Clinton popularity poll. (1998, August 14). *CBS Evening News.* CBS News, New York.

Ritchie, Joy, & Ronald, Kate (Eds.). (2001*). Available Means: An Anthology of Women's Rhetoric(s).* Pittsburgh: University of Pittsburgh Press.

Rosnow, Ralph L., & Robinson, Edward J. (Eds.). (1967). *Experiments in Persuasion* (195–196). New York: Academic Press.

Schlossberg, Caroline Kennedy. (2000, August 15). Speech delivered to the Democratic National Convention. *C-SPAN.*

Serano, Nancy. (2001, March). Charmed, I'm Sure. *Elle,* 302–303.

Sigelman, Lee, Sigelman, Carol, & Fowler, Christopher. (1987). A Bird of a Different Feather? An Experimental Investigation of Physical Attractiveness and the Electability of Female Candidates. *Social Psychology Quarterly, 50,* 32–43.

Tannen, Deborah. (1998). *The Argument Culture: Moving From Debate to Dialogue.* New York: Random House.

Voters Describe Tipper Gore's Appeal as "Real." (2000, September 24). *Greensboro News & Record,* A10.

Watson, Martha Solomon. (1995, October 13). *Autobiography as Rhetorical Discourse.* Spotlight Program: A Discussion with Martha

Solomon Watson. Carolinas Speech Communication Association, Charlotte, NC.

Watson, Martha. (1999). *Lives of Their Own: Rhetorical Dimensions in Autobiographies of Women Activists*. Columbia, SC: University of South Carolina Press.

Wattleton, Faye. (1991). Reproductive Freedom: Fundamental to All Human Rights. In Owen Peterson (Ed.), *Representative American Speeches 1990–91, Vol. 63* (125–131). New York: H. W. Wilson Co.

Wattleton, Faye. (1994). Address at the Triennial Convention of the YWCA. In Victoria L. DeFrancisco & Marvin D. Jensen (Eds.), *Women's Voices in Our Time: Statements by American Leaders* (129–135). Prospect Heights, IL: Waveland Press.

Wattleton, Faye. (1996). *Life on the Line*. New York: Ballantine Books.

Chapter Three: Delivering the Message

American Association of University Women (AAUW). (1991). *Shortchanging Girls, Shortchanging America: Executive Summary*. Washington, DC: Author.

AAUW. (1992). *How Schools Shortchange Girls*. Washington, DC: Author.

Austin, Nancy. (1996, October). Q/A Column. *Presentations, 18*.

Bedard, Paul, Parker, Suzi, Kaplan, David E., & Newman, Richard J. (2000). Fear of Flying? *U.S. News & World Report, 129*, 10.

Bradley, Patricia Hayes. (1981). The Folk-Linguistics of Women's Speech: An Empirical Investigation. *Communication Monographs, 48*, 73–90.

Carli, Linda L. (1990). Gender, Language, and Influence. *Journal of Personality and Social Psychology, 59*, 941–951.

Carli, Linda L, LaFleur, Suzanne J., & Loeber, Christopher, C. (1995). Nonverbal Behavior, Gender, and Influence. *Journal of Personality and Social Psychology, 68*, 1030–1041.

Cohen, Richard. (1997, August 31). When Looks Can Wound. *The Washington Post*, 5.

Cropper, Carol Marie. (1998, October 22). What is the Sound of One Voice-Over Actor Yapping? *The New York Times*, C1.

Dole, Elizabeth. (1996, August 22). Speech delivered at Dole/Kemp Rally. Koury Convention Center, Greensboro, NC.

Eisenberg, Anne. (2000, October 12). Mars and Venus, Online. *The New York Times*, G1ff.

Henley, Nancy. (1977). *Body Politics: Power, Sex and Nonverbal Communication*. New York: Prentice-Hall.

Ireland, Patricia. (1996). *What Women Want*. New York: Dutton.

Jamieson, Kathleen Hall. (1988). *Eloquence in an Electronic Age: The Transformation of Political Speechmaking*. New York: Oxford University Press.

Johnson, Robert. (1994). Young Voices Lost. *Women and Language, 17,* 40–43.

Leathers, Dale G. (1992). *Successful Nonverbal Communication: Principles and Applications* (2nd ed.). New York: MacMillan Publishing Co.

Managing in the Next Millennium: Does Casual Clash With Success? Some Women and Minorities Worry That Relaxed Attire Hurts Professional Image. (1996, March 25). *The Los Angeles Times,* 11.

McCroskey, James C., Simpson, Timothy J., & Richmond, Virginia P. (1982). Biological Sex and Communication Apprehension. *Communication Quarterly, 30,* 129–133.

McPherson, William. (1997). "Dressing Down" in the Business Communication Curriculum. *Business Communication Quarterly, 60,* 134–147.

Mills, J., & Aronson, E. (1965). Opinion Change as a Function of the Communicator's Attractiveness and Desire to Influence. *Journal of Personality and Social Psychology, 1,* 173–177.

Molinari, Susan. (1996, August 13). Keynote Speech to the Republican National Convention. San Diego, CA. *CBS News.*

National Women's Political Caucus. (1995). *Campaigning to Win: The NWPC Guide to Running a Winning Campaign.* Washington, DC: Author.

Newman, Judith. (1997, January/February). Stand up Straight. *Health,* 80–84.

Pearson, Judy C, Turner, Lynn, & Todd-Mancillas, William. (1991). *Gender and Communication* (2nd ed.). Dubuque, IA: Wm. C. Brown Publishers.

Pipher, Mary. (1994). *Reviving Ophelia: Saving the Souls of Adolescents.* New York: Ballantine.

Reich, Robert. (1997, April 17). Interview with Terri Gross. *Fresh Air.* Washington, D.C.: National Public Radio.

Richmond, Virginia P., & McCroskey, James C. (1985). *Communication: Apprehension, Avoidance, and Effectiveness.* Scottsdale, AZ: Gorsuch, Scarisbrick Publishers.

Scaredy Cats. (1997). *American Demographics, 19,* 38.

Screen Actors Guild Campaign. (1996). *Executive Female, 19,* 30.

Serano, Nancy. (2001, March). Charmed, I'm Sure. *Elle,* 302–303.

Sigelman, Lee, Sigelman, Carol, & Fowler, Christopher. (1987). A Bird of a Different Feather? An Experimental Investigation of Physical Attractiveness and the Electability of Female Candidates. *Social Psychology Quarterly, 50,* 32–43.

Stowell, Jessica, & Furlong, Cathy. (1995, November*). Preliminary Findings on Gender Based Fear Reactions in Communication: Apprehension Writings.* Paper presented at the meeting of the Speech Communication Association, San Antonio, TX.

Tannen, Deborah. (1994). *Talking From 9 to 5*. New York: William Morrow.

Tannen, Deborah. (2001, August 28). Workplace Communication. Professional Development Workshop delivered to Montgomery College, Rockville Campus, MD.

Wood, Julia (2003). *Gendered Lives: Communication, Gender, and Culture* (5th ed.). Belmont, CA: Wadsworth.

Chapter Four: Tools of the Trade: Delivery Resources

American Association of University Women (AAUW). (2000). *Tech Savvy: Educating Girls in the New Computer Age: Executive Summary*. http://www.aauw.org. [accessed September 10, 2001].

Barreca, Regina. (1991). *They Used to Call Me Snow White . . . But I Drifted: Women's Strategic Use of Humor*. New York: Penguin Books.

Bauer, John F. (2000, November). *A Technology Gender Divide: Perceived Skill and Frustration Levels Among Female Preservice Teachers*. Paper presented at the meeting of the Educational Research Association. (ERIC Document Reproduction Service No. ED447137).

Benning, Victoria. (1998, July 14). Gender Gap in Fairfax Computer Classes. *The Washington Post*, B1, B5.

Bradley, Patricia H. (1981). Folk-Linguistics of Women's Speech: An Empirical Investigation. *Communication Monographs, 48*, 73–90.

Brosnan, M. (1998). The Impact of Psychological Gender, Gender-Related Perceptions, Significant Others, and the Introducer of Technology Upon Computer Anxiety Among Students. *Journal of Educational Computing Research, 18*, 63–78.

Carli, Linda L. (1990). Gender, Language, and Influence. *Journal of Personality and Social Psychology, 59*, 941–951.

Clinton, Hillary Rodham. (1996, August 27). Speech to the Democratic National Convention. Chicago, IL: *CBS News*.

Crawford, Mary. (1995). *Talking Difference: On Gender and Language*. Thousand Oaks, CA: Sage.

Dyson, Esther. (1999, May 16). The Sound of the Virtual Voice. *The New York Times Magazine*, 44–45.

Edwards, Paul. (1990). Politics of Gender. *Signs, 16*, 102–126.

Ganzel, Rebecca. (2000, February). Power Pointless. *Presentations*, 53–58.

Griffin, Robert, Pettersson, Rune, & Johnson, Ronald. (1997). *The Electronic Presentation: A Status Report of International Use* (Report No. IR 018 353). VisionQuest: Journeys Toward Visual Literacy. Selected Readings From the Annual Conference of the International Visual Literacy Association, Cheyenne, WY. (ERIC Document Reproduction Service No. ED408999).

Gutin, Myra G. (1989). *The President's Partner: The First Lady in the Twentieth Century*. Westport, CT: Greenwood Press.

Hanke, Jon. (1997, May). Innovative Videowall Applications Demonstrate the Power of the Cube. *Presentations,* 53–58.

Hansen, Debra Gold, & Irvin, Sheri D. (1996). Interactive Video and Female Learning: Implications for a Feminized Profession. *Feminist Collections, 17,* 13–15.

Headlam, Bruce. (2000, January 20). Barbie PC: Fashion Over Logic. *The New York Times,* G4ff.

Heimes, Scott. (1997a, June). New Presentations Industry is Evolving from the AV Past. *Presentations,* 8.

Heimes, Scott. (1997b, June). The Future of Projection Technology. *Presentations,* 31–35.

Jaffe, Clella. (2001). *Public Speaking: A Cultural Perspective* (3rd ed.). Belmont, CA: Wadsworth Publishing Company.

Jaffe, Greg. (2000, April 26). What's Your Point, Lieutenant? Just Cut to the Pie Charts—The Pentagon Declares War on Electronic Slide Shows That Make Briefings a Pain. *The Wall Street Journal,* A1.

Kearney, Patricia, & Plax, Timothy G. (1999). *Public Speaking in a Diverse Society* (2nd ed.). Mountain View, CA: Mayfield Publishing.

Keogh, Teresa, Barnes, Peter, Joiner, Richard, & Littleton, Karen. (2000). Gender, Pair Composition and Computer Versus Paper Presentations of an English Language Task. *Educational Psychology, 20,* 33–44.

Maney, Kevin. (1999, May 12). PowerPoint Obsession Takes Off. *USA Today.* http://www.usatoday.com/life/tech/ctfl44.htm. [accessed July 17, 2001].

Morse, F. K., & Daiute, C. (1992). *I LIKE Computers Versus I LIKERT Computers: Rethinking Methods for Assessing the Gender Gap in Computing.* Cambridge, MA: Harvard University and Apple Computer. (ERIC Document Reproduction Service No. ED 349 939).

Mrs. Hoover Takes Voice Test to Improve Talkie Technique. (1931, November 6). *The New York Times,* 4.

Mulac, Anthony. (1998). The Gender-Linked Language Effect: Do Language Differences Really Make a Difference? In D. J. Canary & K. Dindia (Eds.), *Sex Differences and Similarities in Communication* (127–153). Mahwah, NJ: Lawrence Erlbaum Associates.

Ogletree, Shirley M., & Williams, Sue W. (1990). Sex and Sex-Typing Effects on Computer Attitudes and Aptitude. *Sex Roles, 23,* 703–712.

Reinen, Ingeborg Janssen, & Plomp, Tjeerd. (1997). Information Technology and Gender Equality: A Contradiction in Terminus? *Computers and Education,* 28, 65–78.

Simon, Bernard. (2002, August 29). WordPerfect Gets New Life in Deal With 2 PC Makers, *The New York Times,* 5.

Steinke, J., & Long, M. (1995). *A Lab of Her Own? Portrayals of Female Characters on Children's Educational Science Programs.*

Washington, D.C.: International Communication Association. (ERIC Document Reproduction Service No. ED 384 937).

Tannen, Deborah. (1994, May 16). Gender Gap in Cyberspace. *Newsweek*, 52–53.

Turkle, Sherry. (1984). *The Second Self: Computers and the Human Spirit*. New York: Simon & Schuster.

Whitley, B. E. (1997). Gender Differences in Computer-Related Attitudes and Behavior: A Meta-Analysis. *Computers in Human Behavior, 13*, 1–22.

Chapter Five: Public Speaking Situations

3M Meeting Network's 1998 On-Line Meeting Survey Results. http://www.3m.com/meetingnetwork/readingroom/survey-results-1998.html. [accessed September 13, 2001].

Caudron, Shari. (1999, May). The Female Profession. *Training and Development*, 54.

Chaplin, William F., Phillips, Jeffrey B., Clanton, Jonathan D., Clanton, Nancy R., & Stein, Jennifer L. (2000). Handshaking, Gender, Personality and First Impression. *Journal of Personality and Social Psychology, 19,* 110–117.

Craig, Robert L. (Ed.). (1996). *The ASTD Training and Development Handbook: A Guidebook to Human Resource Development* (4th ed.). New York: McGraw-Hill.

DiSanza, James. (1998, March 31). On the Importance of Public Speaking. CRTNET NEWS [NCA Listserve], No. 2780. Available by email: crtnet@natcom.org.

Fick-Cooper, Lynn. (1997, September 27). Toast to the bride and groom. Greensboro, NC.

Gerhart, Ann. (2001, September 18). Laura Bush, Comforter in Chief. *The Washington Post.* http://www.washingtonpost.com/wp-dyn/articles/A52751-2001Sep18.html. [accessed September 19, 2001].

Johnson, John R., & Szczupakiewicz, Nancy. (1987). The Public Speaking Course: Is it Preparing Students with Work Related Public Speaking Skills? *Communication Education, 36,* 131–137.

Kirby, Andy. (1995). *Great Games for Trainers*. Amherst, MA: HRD Press.

Mager, Robert F. (1997). *Preparing Instructional Objectives* (3rd ed.). Atlanta: Center for Effective Performance.

Newstrom, John W., Scannell, Edward E., & Nilson, Carolyn D. (1998). *The Complete Games Trainers Play, Volume II*. New York: McGraw-Hill.

Petrin, Catherine. (1993, July). A Six-Pack of Skills for Success. *Training & Development*, 12.

Silberman, Mel (Ed.). (2002). *The 2002 Training & Performance Sourcebook.* New York: McGraw-Hill.

U.S. Businesses Pay the Price for "Meeting Mania." (1999, May). *Public Relations Tactics,* 20.

Wakeman, Mary Kaye. (1997, March 15). Introduction of Keynote Speaker delivered to Women's Studies Conference, University of North Carolina, Greensboro, NC.

West, Edie. (1999). *The Big Book of Icebreakers: Quick, Fun Activities for Energizing Meetings and Workshops.* New York: McGraw-Hill.

Zielinski, Dave. (1998, August). Do Women Have to be Better Presenters Than Men? *Presentations.* http://presentations.com. [accessed November 5, 1998].

Chapter Six: Woman as Public Persona

Anderson, Karrin Vasby. (forthcoming). The First Lady as a Site of "American Womanhood." In Molly M. Wertheimer (Ed.), *Inventing Their Voices: The Rhetoric of American First Ladies of the Twentieth Century.* New York: Rowman and Littlefield.

Aristotle. (1943). Politics (Benjamin Jowett, Trans.). In L.R. Loomis (Ed.), *On Man in the Universe* (267–269). Roslyn, NY: Walter J. Black, Inc.

Blankenship, Jane, & Robson, Deborah C. (1995). A "Feminine Style" in Women's Political Discourse: An Exploratory Essay. *Communication Quarterly, 43,* 353–366.

Brubach, Holly. (1996, November 24). Heroine Worship: The Age of the Female Icon. *The New York Times Magazine,* 55–57.

Bumiller, Elisabeth. (1997, November 2). The Politics of Personality. *The New York Times Magazine,* 36–39.

Bush's Top Female Aide Has Clout, Home Life. (2001, April 15). *Greensboro News & Record,* A7.

First Lady Hillary Clinton. (1997, January 19). *CBS Sunday Morning.* New York: CBS News.

Chisholm, Shirley. (1997, January 29). Keynote Speech at 11th Annual MLK, Jr. Celebration Program. University of North Carolina, Greensboro, NC.

Cortina, Lilia M., Swan, Suzanne, Fitzgerald, Louise F., & Waldo, Craig. (1998). Sexual Harassment and Assault: Chilling the Climate for Women in Academia. *Psychology of Women Quarterly, 22,* 419–441.

Definition of *persona.* (1992). *The American Heritage Dictionary* (3rd. ed.) (1351). Boston: Houghton Mifflin Company.

Dreifus, Claudia. (1994, January 30). Joycelyn Elders. *The New York Times Magazine,* 16–19.

Dobbs, Michael. (1997, June 15). Albright Reshapes Role of Nation's Top Diplomat. *The Washington Post,* A1, A10, A11.

First Lady Drawing Admiration for Strength. (1998, August 29). *Greensboro News & Record*, A5.

Gibbs, Nancy, & Duffy, Michael. (1996, July 1). Just Heartbeats Away. *Time*, 24–28.

Goodnough, Abby. (1997, September 14). Susan Molinari, Out of Congress and on Camera, *The New York Times* (national edition), 39.

Gold, Ellen Reid, & Speicher, Renee. (1995). Marilyn Quayle Meets the Press: Marilyn Loses. *The Southern Communication Journal, 61*, 93–103.

Jamieson, Kathleen Hall. (1988). *Eloquence in an Electronic Age: The Transformation of Political Speechmaking.* New York: Oxford University Press.

Jamieson, Kathleen Hall. (1996a, November 11). *Lessons of the '96 Campaign.* Harriett Elliott Lecture delivered at the University of North Carolina, Greensboro, NC.

Jamieson, Kathleen Hall. (1996b, November 12). Personal conversation with Professor Natalle.

Johnson, Allen H. (2002, June 2). Johnnetta Cole and the Lyrical Gospel of Bennett's Survival. *Greensboro News & Record*, H2.

Johnson, Samuel. (1929). In Woolf, Virginia. *A Room of One's Own* (56). New York: Harvest, HBJ.

Johnston, David, & Sontag, Deborah. (1997, November 23). Reno's Loner Image Belies a More Complex Reality, *The New York Times* (national edition), 1, 12.

Kelly, Christine, Laffoon, E. Anne, & McKerrow, Raymie E. (1994). *Diversity in Public Communication: A Reader.* Dubuque, IA: Kendall/Hunt Publishing Company.

Knowles-Borishade, Adetokunbo. (1994). Paradigm for Classical African Orature. In Kelly, Christine, Laffoon, E. Anne, & McKerrow, Raymie E. (Eds.), *Diversity in Public Communication: A Reader.* (94–102). Dubuque, IA: Kendall/Hunt Publishing Company.

Laura Bush Wins Wide Approval. (2001, July 25). *Greensboro News & Record*, A2.

Lederer, Edith M. (1997, December 26). Queen Gets Personal in Holiday Message, *Greensboro News & Record*, A1, A2.

Liswood, Laura A. (1995). *Women World Leaders: Fifteen Great Politicians Tell Their Stories.* London: Pandora/HarperCollins Publishers.

Molinari, Susan. (1998). *Representative Mom.* New York: Doubleday.

Mundy, Liza. (1998, January 25). Punch Lines: What is it About Janet Reno That So Fascinates and Confounds and Even Terrifies America? *The Washington Post Magazine*, 7–11, 21–25.

National Women's Political Caucus. (1995). *Campaigning to Win: The NWPC Guide to Running a Winning Campaign.* Washington, DC:

Author.

Newsom, Doug, & Carrell, Bob. (2001). *Public Relations Writing: Form and Style.* Belmont, CA: Wadsworth Publishers.

Palczewski, Catherine Helen. (1996). Argumentation and Feminisms: An Introduction. *Argumentation and Advocacy, 32,* 161–169.

Purdum, Todd S. (1996, August 25). Advisers See a Bright Side to Criticism of First Lady, *The New York Times,* 1, 13.

Rather, Dan. (1996, August 13). Coverage of the Republican National Convention keynote speech. *CBS News.*

Reed, Julia. (2001, October). The President's Prodigy. *Vogue,* 396–403, 448–449.

Reno, Janet. (1999, March 28). Interview with Rita Braver. *CBS Sunday Morning.* New York: CBS News.

Rice, Condoleezza. (2000, August 1). Speech to the Republican National Convention, Philadelphia, PA. *C-SPAN.*

Ritchie, Joy, & Ronald, Kate (Eds.). (2001*). Available Means: An Anthology of Women's Rhetoric(s).* Pittsburgh: University of Pittsburgh Press.

Roberts, Cokie. (1998). *We Are Our Mothers' Daughters.* New York: William Morrow and Company, Inc.

Sanger, David E., Shanker, Thom, & Perlez, Jane. (2001, September 23). From Many Voices, a New War Council. *The New York Times* (national edition), A1, B2.

Sigma Gamma Rho Sorority, Inc. (2002, November 14). *S.I.S.T.E.R.S.: Sigmas Inspiring Sisters to Educate and Self Respect. A Historical and Contemporary Examination of Issues Amongst Women of Color.* Program from a forum sponsored by the Omicron Eta Chapter of Sigma Gamma Rho Sorority, Inc. and held at the University of North Carolina at Greensboro, Greensboro, NC.

Stengel, Richard. (1996, July 1). Liddy Makes Perfect, *Time,* 30–33, 36–39.

1 Timothy, Chapter 2, Verse 11.12, KJV.

Truman, Margaret. (1995). *First Ladies.* New York: Random House.

Zook, Krystal Brent. (1995, November 12). A Manifesto of Sorts for a Black Feminist Movement, *The New York Times Magazine,* 85–89.

Epilogue

The Freedom Forum & ADT Research. (1998, October 20). Who Speaks For America? Sex, Age and Race on the Network News. http://www.freedomforum.org/templates/document.asp?document ID=6403. [accessed September 25, 2001].

Pullout Tools

**Pullout Tool
Presentation Checklist**

Setting a Goal

1. _____ Did you select a specific goal? In other words, can you answer specifically the question: "What do I want my audience to know or be able to do at the end of my presentation?"

Preparation

2. _____ Do you know your audience? What is their educational level? Knowledge of the topic? Age? Socioeconomic background? (See the pullout tool on audience analysis for more in-depth analysis if you need it.)

3. _____ Have you considered the occasion, situation, or environment as a significant influence on your speech content?

4. _____ Does the presentation begin with an interesting, attention-getting introduction and a very brief preview of the main points?

5. _____ Does the organizational format best reflect the speech content (for example, chronological for time-based topic or problem-solution for problem solving persuasion)?

6. _____ Is there adequate supporting material or evidence for each main point?

7. _____ Are there stories or other interactive devices to engage the audience?

8. _____ Does the presentation end with a summary of the main points and a creative finishing touch?

9. _____ Are transitions planned between each of the major points?

10. _____ Have all facts and data been doubled-checked for accuracy?

11. _____ Have you planned a method of evaluation? How will you know the audience has understood your intent?

Delivery

12. _____ Did you practice the presentation aloud between five and ten times?

13. _____ Did you practice using your visual aids during rehearsal?

14. _____ Did you time the presentation at least three times?

15. _____ Did you visit the room or auditorium where the presentation will take place?

16. _____ Did you check all the equipment to make sure it is working properly? Do you have a back-up plan for failed or forgotten equipment and visual aids?

17. _____ Have you prepared a set of brief notes to take to the podium?

18. _____ Has the proper pronunciation of all key words been determined?

19. _____ Are you wearing something appropriate to the audience and occasion, as well as something that is comfortable and makes you feel confident?

20. _____ Are you now ready to take a deep breath and smile just at the time of your presentation?

Pullout Tool
Speech Outline Template

Title:

_____

_____

Specific Goal: At the end of my speech, I want my audience to

_____

_____

Introduction: (Attention grabber)

_____

_____

(Thesis—see specific goal above and reword in appropriate language for the audience)

_____

_____

(Preview of Main Points)

_____

_____

*Transition:*_____

_____

Body:

I. First Main Idea

_____

_____

A. Supporting Material (Story, Statistic, Quotation, etc.)

_____

_____

B. Supporting Material (Story, Statistic, Quotation, etc.)

_____

_____

C. Supporting Material (Story, Statistic, Quotation, etc.)

_____

_____

*Transition:*_____

_____

II. Second Main Idea

_____

_____

A. Supporting Material (Story, Statistic, Quotation, etc.)

_____

_____

B. Supporting Material (Story, Statistic, Quotation, etc.)

_____

_____

C. Supporting Material (Story, Statistic, Quotation, etc.)

_____

_____

*Transition:*_____

_____

III. Third Main Idea

_____

_____

    A. Supporting Material (Story, Statistic, Quotation, etc.)

_____

_____

    B. Supporting Materia (Story, Statistic, Quotation, etc.)

_____

_____

    C. Supporting Material (Story, Statistic, Quotation, etc.)

_____

_____

*Transition:*_____

_____

Conclusion: (Summary of Main Points)

_____

_____

(Creative Finish/Call to Action)

_____

_____

Pullout Tool
Audience Analysis Checklist

A checklist can become a mental habit after a time. If you are unfamiliar with audience analysis, use the following questions to get started.

_____ How many people will be in attendance?

_____ Are they male or female? Proportion of male to female?

_____ What is the age range?

_____ What is the racial or ethnic makeup of the audience?

_____ What is the socioeconomic status of the group in general?

_____ What is the level of education or preparedness for this topic?

_____ What is the predominant religious affiliation of this audience?

_____ Is this a professional group or a lay audience?

_____ What attitudes toward the speaker or topic is the audience likely to have?

_____ How will the audience be seated during the event?

_____ What other aspects of the physical environment may affect the audience?

_____ Where is my speech in the sequence of events?

_____ How will the occasion affect the mind-set of the audience?

_____ What political party do the majority of audience members belong to?

_____ What stories will appeal to the audience? How can we connect?

Notes:

Pull Out Tool
Sources for Further Study

In addition to following up on resources listed in the bibliography, there are some typical resources that you can read on a regular basis to enhance your own public speaking. Read the Sunday edition of a large city newspaper such as the *New York Times* or the *Washington Post*. This will put you in touch with the pulse of the nation. Read biographies and autobiographies of women in the public eye or historical figures. Aspects of their public speaking styles and personas are often illuminated. Go listen to speakers when you have the opportunity. Many public figures speak at universities and colleges where admission to such an event is usually free. Study the speeches of successful women by regularly checking *Vital Speeches of the Day*.

Below, we have provided three groups of reference citations: the first is a sample of the wide range of speeches that are available for your review, the second is a list of quotable resources, and the third is a list of web sites to assist you in constructing your speeches.

Speeches for Further Reading and Study

Koellner, Laurette. (2001, January 15). Managing Your Career: The Ultimate Solo Flight. *Vital Speeches of the Day,* 213–216.

Mackay-Lassonde, Claudette. (1996, July 1). Let's Stop Fooling Ourselves: No Man or Woman Can Have It All. *Vital Speeches of the Day,* 569–571.

Mathews, Jessica. (1990). Man & Nature: The Future of Global Environment. In C.M. Logue & J. Dehart (Eds.), *Representative American Speeches 1990-1991,* 58–68.

Nix, S. Michelle. (2000). *Women at the Podium: Memorable Speeches in History.* New York: HarperCollins.

Opheim, Cynthia. (2000, November 1). Making Democracy Work: Your Responsibility to Society. *Vital Speeches of the Day,* 60–61.

Richardson, Margaret Milner. (1995, January 15). Taxation with Representation: 2001 and Beyond. *Vital Speeches of the Day,* 201–203.

Ritchie, Joy & Ronald, Kate (2001). *Available Means: An Anthology of Women's Rhetoric(s).* Pittsburgh: University of Pittsburgh Press.

Sarkela, Sandra J., Ross, Susan M., & Lowe, Margaret A. (2003). *From Megaphones to Microphones: Speeches of American Women, 1920–1960.* Westport, CT: Praeger.

Scherer, Karla. (1990, September 1). Corporate Power: Some Facts They Never Teach You in the Classroom. *Vital Speeches of the Day,* 679–681.

Schultz, Deborah E. (1987, April 1). What Do You Want to Know Late in the Twentieth Century? How Can You Know It? *Vital Speeches of the Day,* 366–368.

Shalala, Donna. (1994, May 15). Domestic Terrorism: An Unacknowledged Epidemic. *Vital Speeches of the Day,* 450–453.

Walters, Farah. (1995, June 1). Successfully Managing Diversity: Why the Right Thing to Do is Also the Smart Thing to Do. *Vital Speeches of the Day,* 496–500.

Weldon, Virginia. (1994, November 15). The Power of Changing the Context: Women in the Workplace. *Vital Speeches of the Day,* 217–219.

Quotable Resources

Anderson, Peggy. (1997). *Great Quotes From Great Women.* Franklin Lakes, NJ: Career Press.

Biggs, Mary. (1996). *Women's Words: The Columbia Book of Quotations by Women.* New York: Columbia University Press.

Kerschen, Lois. (1998). *American Proverbs About Women: A Reference Guide.* Westport, CT: Greenwood Press.

Maggio, Rosalie. (1996). *The New Beacon Book of Quotations by Women.* Boston: Beacon Press.

Quinn, Tracy. (Ed.). (1999). *Quotable Women of the 20th Century.* New York: William Morrow.

Warner, Carolyn. (1992). *The Last Word: A Treasury of Women's Quotes.* Englewood Cliffs, NJ: Prentice Hall.

Web Sites to Assist in Speech Construction

Gifts of Speech (Sweet Briar College) web site: http://gos.sbc.edu/

Grammar and Gender Bibliography web site: http://ccat.sas.upenn.edu/~haroldfs/popcult/bibliogs/gender/genderbib.htm

The Ladies Room web site:
http://www.geocities.com/Wellesley/2052/genddiff.html

Presentations magazine web site: http://www.presentations.com

Journal Notes

Journal Notes

Index

After the speech, 69–71
African American, *see Race*
Albright, Madeleine, 5–6, 40–42, 132
Appearance, *see also Clothing*
    audience views on, 40–43
    and posture, 64
    and self-esteem, 56
    on television, 86–87
Apprehension, *see Fear*
Analysis
    of audience, 24–39
    of self, 11, 39, 71
Anxiety, *see Fear*
Audience
    creating relevance for, 26
    diversity of, 24–25
    emotional response of, 32–38, 45–46
    feedback from, 43, 110–11
    first impressions from, 50
    focus on, 57–58
    hostile, 31–38
    individual contact with, 26–27
    interaction with, 43–48
    mind-set of, 31
    networking, 47
    participation, 28, 43–48
    persona's effect on, 37–38
    rapport with, 26–27, 38–39
    relating to, 23–48
    sensitivity of, 90, 92–93
Audience, connection to
    with business cards, 47
    creating, 20, 23, 38–39, 42–43, 67–68
    by eye contact, 38, 67
    fear of loosing, 19
    maintaining, 38–39, 67–68, 71
    with narrative, 28–31
    and overt involvement, 44–45
    and versatility, 46–47
Audience analysis
    checklist for, 24, 160
    depth of, 27
    nontraditional, 28–31
    on-the-spot, 110
    for panel speaking, 103
    and rapport, 26–27, 39
    research for, 23–26, 103
    traditional, 25–28
Audience expectations
    discovering, 24–25
    of interaction, 47–48
    of gender, 51–52, 89
    and mind-set, 31
    of personal appearance, 40–43
    regarding occasion, 31
    and stereotypes, 25, 32–33
Austin, Nancy, and physical appearance, 50, 62–63
Autobiography, 29
Awards, 99–101

Bodenheimer, Fritzi, biography of, 10
Boomerang effect, 34–35
Breathing, 65
Bush, Laura, 31, 95, 122
Business speaking, *see Workplace*
Business cards, 47

Campaigning, 117-19
Casual Friday, 60–61
Cell phones, 45
Challenges
    of gender, 16
    of misogyny, 116–17
    of racism, 125–26
    of sexism, 33, 114–17
Charm, power of, 42
Chrisholm, Shirley, 31, 126–27
Clinton, Hillary Rodham, 34–35, 90–91, 115, 119–22
Clothing
    conformance of, 62–63
    and credibility, 59–61
    distracting, 62
    expectations of, 40–43, 60
    as investment, 61–62
    judgments of, 59–60
    and persona, 62–63
    planning of, 60
    and race, 129
    and reputation, 40–43
    selecting, 60–63, 69, 81, 84
Communication
    cultural effect on, 32
    gender differences in, 77–79
    feminine style of, 15–16, 20–21, 109, 117–18
    masculine style of, 15, 18
    nonverbal, 66–68
Computers
    anxiety toward, 75
    and gender differences, 75–78
    and stereotypes, 75–77
    and visual aids, 81–84
Concluding a speech, 70–71

Confidence
  building, 57
  and posture, 64
Controversy, 36–37
Conversational style, 45
Crawford, Mary, gender research of, 14–15, 90
Credibility
  building, 52
  and clothing, 59–61, 129
  and gender, 50–52
  maintaining, 67, 71, 90, 106
  and visual aids, 81–83

Delivery
  posture during, 64
  rehearsal of, 52–53, 58–59, 68, 97–98, 103
  of reports, 106–7
  resources, 73–93
  stages of, 49
  voice during, 65–66
Demographics, 23
Diversity, 24
Dole, Elizabeth
  audience connection to, 29, 41–42, 45, 67
  cartoon of, 6
  charm of, 42
  personal appearance of, 41–42
  as role model, 5

Elders, Joycelyn, and race, 124–26
Evaluation, *see Self-Evaluation*
Evers–Williams, Myrlie, 42, 128
Eye contact
  maintaining, 66–67
  and rapport, 38, 45

Facets of public speaking, 7
Faludi, Susan, on fear, 4, 13
Fear
  controlling, 56–59
  and female mind-set, 3–4, 53–55
  of first experience, 54
  and gender differences, 3–4, 54–55
  toward persuasion, 19
  and pitch, 65
  realistic expectations of, 58
  reducing, 14, 53, 58
  and self-esteem, 4, 55–56
  of technology, 74–79
  of television cameras, 85
  and visualization, 58
Fee, requesting, 103
Feedback, 43, 50

Feminine
  definition of, 17, 51–52
  style, 15–16, 20–21, 109, 117–19
Feminist theory of rhetoric, 20
Ferraro, Geraldine, 27–28, 37
Finishing a speech, 70–71
First ladies, 119–22
Fisher, Mary, 33–34, 46
Flipcharts, 81
Foss, Karen, on communication, 16, 20
Foss, Sonja, on rhetoric, 16, 20

Gender
  challenges of, 16
  and credibility, 50–52
  definition of, 17
  as personality, 25
  in politics, 115–34
  and respect, 50
  social effects on, 17
  and status, 51
  stereotypes of, 17, 25, 32–33, 51–52
  and technology, 74–79
Gender differences
  and fear, 3–4, 54–55
  in humor, 90
  in self-esteem, 4, 56
  and style, 14–16
  in workplace, 105
Gender identity politics, 133–34

Handshake, 100
History
  of handbooks, 1
  stereotypes from, 51, 114–17
  of women in public, 114–17
Hostile audience
  and boomerang effect, 34–35
  counteracting, 37–38
  dialogue with, 36–38
  handling a, 32–35
  preparing for, 34, 36–37, 58
  realistic expectations of, 33
  recognizing, 32–33
  rhetoric for, 36–37
  and sexism, 33, 114–17
Humor, 43–44, 90–91

Immediacy, 67–68
Interaction
  with audience, 43–48
  and cell phones, 45
  with conversational style, 45
  diplomacy in, 46–47

feedback as, 43
following speech, 71
with humor, 43–44
internal, 45–46
mistakes in, 47–48
overt, 43–45
as panel speaker, 102–5
over time, 46–48
Interview, on television, 87–88
Introducing speakers, 96–99, 104–5
Invitations to speak, 102–3
Invitational rhetoric, 20
Ireland, Patricia, former president of NOW, 37, 54, 115

Jamieson, Kathleen Hall, 15–16, 51, 115, 131–32
Jokes, *see Humor*

Kennedy, Jacqueline, 40, 42, 119
King, Coretta Scott, 5, 128

Language
    sensitivity in, 88
    gender differences in, 89–92
    and humor, 90–91
    politically correct, 92–93
    qualifiers in, 91–92
    and word choice, 88, 92
    vagueness of, 93

Masculine
    definition of, 17, 51–52
    style, 15, 18
Media, 129–33
Media image
    counteracting, 37–38
    creating, 63, 127–135
Meetings, 107–8
Microphones, 45, 83–85, 140
Moderator, 103–5
Molinari, Susan, 65, 116
Murray, Patty, media image of, 127–28, 134

Narrative
    autobiography as, 29–31
    efficacy of, 30–31, 36
    sincerity of, 31
    style, 20–21
    types of, 21
Natalle, Elizabeth "Jody," biography of, 9–10
Nervousness, *see Fear*

Objectification of women, 114–17
Occasion, *see also Setting, Situation*
    award ceremony as, 99–101
    audience expectations of, 31
    business meeting as, 107–8
    introductions as, 96–99
    and time, 46–47
    toast as, 101–2
    training as, 108–11
Opportunities
    and business cards, 47
    creating future, 47
    variety of, 7
Organization
    agonistic style of, 15
    Aristotelian style of, 15
    feminine approach to, 15–16
    linear approach to, 15, 18
    masculine approach to, 15
    for meetings, 107–8
    need for, 14
    nonlinear approach to, 16
    personalizing, 20
Outline template, 157–59
Overhead projector, 80

Palczewski, Catherine Helen, research of, 3, 134
Panel speaking, 102–5
Persona
    and clothing, 62–63
    conforming, 63, 127–28
    definition of, 113
    factors of, 128–29
    and media image, 120, 128
    misunderstood, 125
    need for, 4–5
    and race, 124–29
    reshaping, 34–35
    successful women with, 5
Persuasion
    and audience analysis, 27–28
    boomerang effect on, 34
    fear toward, 19
    and gender, 18, 25, 32–33, 52
    indirect approach to, 19–20
    interpersonal quality of, 20
    perception of, 19
    realistic expectations of, 33
    and status, 52
    structure of, 20
    tentative style of, 91–92
Physical space
    and audience, 103
    in giving or receiving awards, 99–100
    and rapport, 38, 39
Pitch, of voice, 65–66, 101

Podium
   approaching, 64
   problems with, 68–69
Politically correct language, 92–93
Politics
   and campaigning, 117–19
   gender identity, 133–34
   public perception of, 2
   women in, 118–27
   women of color in, 124–27
Posture, 64, 99–100
PowerPoint, 76–78, 81–83
Practice, *see* Rehearsal
Preparation
   audience analysis in, 23–48
   of clothing, 60
   contacting audience members as, 27
   to give an award, 99–100
   for hostile audience, 32–34, 36–37, 58
   for introductions, 96–97, 104
   and knowing topic, 57
   organization as part of, 18
   for problems, 69–70
   to receive award, 100–101
   selecting material as, 30–31
   speaking aloud for, 52–53
   for a toast, 101
   for training, 110–11
   and voice, 58–59
Presentation checklist, 155–56
Press, *see* Media
Prime Ministers, 122–24
Princess Diana, 123
Public Image, *see* Media image
Public speaking
   facets of, 6
   feminine style of, 15–16, 20–21, 109, 117–19
   masculine style of, 15, 18

Queen Elizabeth, 69, 122–23
Question and Answer (Q&A)
   as audience interaction, 46
   and hostile audience, 69–71
   managing, 70–71
   tips on, 72
Race
   expectations of, 129
   and self-esteem, 56
   and persona, 124–29
   in politics, 124–28
Rapport
   and appearance, 40–43, 48
   and audience analysis, 39
   creating, 38, 67–68

   and humor, 43–44
   maintaining, 67–68
   mistakes creating, 47–48
   and physical space, 38
   and time, 46–48
Reflection, self, 11, 71
Rehearsal
   and physical delivery, 53, 68
   of introductions, 97–98
   as panel speaker, 103
   to reduce fear, 53
   speaking aloud during, 52–53
   at venue, 53
   with visual aids, 53
Reports, 106–7
Rhetoric
   definition of, 17–18
   feminine style of, 15–16, 20–21, 117–19
   feminist theory of, 20
   for hostile audience, 36–37
Rice, Condoleezza, 5, 122, 127

Self-Esteem, 4, 55–56
Self-Evaluation
   on creating rapport, 39
   on speaking ability, 11
   after speaking, 71
Setting, *see also* Occasion
   award ceremony, 99–101
   business meeting, 107–8
   classroom, 108–11
   panel, 102–5
   training, 108–11
   workplace, 105–11
Sexism
   and hostile audience, 33
   problem of, 33, 114–17
Shoes, 61, 69
Sincerity, 31
Situations, *see* Occasion, Setting
   award ceremony, 99–101
   business meeting, 107–8
   giving reports, 106–7
   introductions, 96–99, 104
   panel speaking, 102–5
   toasts, 101–2
   training, 108–11
Smiling, 64–65, 67
Software, visual
   and PowerPoint, 81
   prevalence of, 79
   variety of, 79
Status
   expectations of, 51–52
   increasing women's, 51–52
   and persona, 120

Steinem, Gloria, 3, 90
Stereotypes
    from audience, 25
    creation of, 51, 55–56
    of gender, 25, 32–33
    from history, 51, 114–16
    from pop culture, 57, 76–77
    self–awareness of, 25
    of voice, 66
Style
    argumentative, 3, 32
    autobiographical, 29
    consensual, 3
    conversational, 45
    developing personal, 18
    feminine, 15–16, 20–21, 109, 117–19
    gender differences of, 15–17, 89–92
    interactive, 45
    masculine, 15, 18
    narrative, 28–31
    range of, 18
    teaching, 16

Tannen, Deborah, 14–15, 32, 77
Technology
    and cell phones, 45
    choosing appropriate, 79–80
    and computers, 75–78, 81–84
    and gender differences, 74–79
    history of problems with, 73
Teleprompters, 85–87
Television
    appearance on, 86–87
    and awards 99–100
    and gender differences, 86
    interviews on, 87–88
    live, 87
    speaking tips for, 86–88
    and teleprompters, 85–87
Terminology, in this book, 17
Thatcher, Margaret, persona of, 123–24
Time
    on panel, 104
    during Q&A, 70–72
    and rapport, 46–48
Toasting, 101–2
Tool
    clothing as, 59–63
    computer as, 81–83
    language as, 88–93
    technological, 81–83
    traditional, 80–81
Training, 108–11
Tweeten, Taresa, 18–20

Visual aids, 53, 78–83
Visualization, 58, 103
Voice
    and breath, 65
    keeping clear, 58–59
    through microphone, 84–85
    as panel speaker, 103
    pitch of, 65–66
    stereotypes of, 66
    during a toast, 101

Wattleton, Faye, 5, 36–37
World leaders, 124
Workplace
    giving reports in, 106–7
    preparing for, 105–11
    training in, 108–11